THE CHALLENGE
OF THE KLAN

THE CHALLENGE
OF THE KLAN

BY

STANLEY FROST

NEGRO UNIVERSITIES PRESS
NEW YORK

Originally published in 1924
by the Bobbs-Merrill Company

Reprinted 1969 by
Negro Universities Press
A DIVISION OF GREENWOOD PUBLISHING CORP.
NEW YORK

Library of Congress Catalogue Card Number 75-94227

SBN 8371-2192-2

PRINTED IN UNITED STATES OF AMERICA

22449

CONTENTS

v

FOREWORD

THIS discussion of the Ku Klux Klan has been written in the belief that the time has come when both enemies and friends of that remarkable organization will wish to know all the facts that can be learned about it, good as well as bad. The movement has reached an importance calling for more than merely partisan knowledge, all good or all bad. This work is therefore, as far as my ability allows, a piece of reporting intended to avoid either judicial or propagandist attitudes and merely presenting the evidence on both sides of the case.

It does assume that in doing this, purposes, motives, "states of mind," and social, economic and historical backgrounds, perspectives and causes are at least as important as those facts which lie on the surface. There are obvious difficulties and possibilities of error and bias in discovering and stating them, but they must nevertheless be included in any report which hopes to be of value. If, in the selection of material, a slight preponderance has been given to the Klan's purposes and defenses, this is not with any desire to favor that body, but because the attacks upon it have

vii

been so many and thorough that too great a threshing of this old straw is sure to become wearisome to any except those who read merely to confirm and cultivate a fixed dislike.

The preparation of the material for publication in book form has permitted considerable additions to the articles which originally appeared in *The Outlook*. While this does not alter the evidence in any vital way, it is both important and interesting. It includes a complete reprint of the Klan's Constitution, considerable excerpts from its published propaganda, and a statement by a leading Klansman of the spiritual and religious side of the movement, with the effect this may have inside the Protestant church organizations. There are, besides, minor corrections due partly to the growth of the Klan and to developments since the articles were first written, and partly 'to information furnished by the many readers who have written to advise, criticize and sometimes commend.

I regret that it is impossible to answer all such letters, to debate with their writers. My answer, however, would be about the same in every case, and I take this opportunity to bring it to the attention of readers of the book. It is that in an organization so large and so amazingly variegated as the Klan almost anything that may be said about it, whether good or bad, is true at some time and in some places. I have told of no sins that are not admitted by its own officers

FOREWORD

except where there is clear proof, and of no virtues not conceded by some of its most vigorous enemies. No fair reporter could do less, nor could he base his reports on any locality or group of localities, as most readers must do of necessity.

The letters I have received do, however, show sharply the need of pointing out not only this mixed quality of the Klan, but its rapid changes. It is growing so fast and is being reformed and developed so rapidly that many facts which were true about it even a year ago have become false, and conclusions based upon them are by now very often invalid. It is certain that modifications will have occurred even between the time this is written and the time it is read!

I can not hope that in making this report I have been able always to be fair, or always to find the whole truth. The one virtue I do claim for the book is that it does give all the essential facts my limited abilities have allowed me to find and is written with a strong desire for fairness. The fact that attack and approval have come with about equal vigor from both sides encourages me to hope that I have been measurably successful.

THE AUTHOR

February 1, 1924.

THE CHALLENGE
OF THE KLAN

THE CHALLENGE OF THE KLAN

CHAPTER I

THE GIANT IN THE WHITE HOOD

THE Ku Klux Klan has become the most vigorous, active and effective organization in American life outside business. Its influence, though intangible and often secret, affects every public question and every activity which depends in any degree on public opinion; its power is incalculable since it is wholly different from that of any other known force. It controls, in a way in which no political party has ever controlled, hundred of cities, towns and counties, a few states; it has elected its picked men mayors, sheriffs and judges, legislators and governors, representatives and senators in Congress. It is reaching for the presidency.

Moreover, it is growing with tremendous speed. Its members are already beyond four millions and are increasing at the rate of a hundred thousand a week. All efforts that have been made to check or destroy it have failed; indeed, they seem only to have speeded its growth. If it is not yet able to impose its will on the nation, it is surely on a road which may soon take it to the place of supreme power. The cloud which two years ago was no bigger than a man's hand has covered a great part of the heavens and is still spreading.

This is the first of the reasons why there should be a new and careful consideration of the Klan. It is a reason which appeals to every man and woman to whom it makes a cent's worth of difference whether their opinions and judgments on public affairs are accurate and well-founded. All such people must from now on know the real facts of the strength, the methods, the habits and the intentions of this white-hooded giant, as well as the dangers his existence creates. All thought regarding the body politic is subject to discount in exact proportion to the lacks and inaccuracies of this information.

But there are other reasons for a re-appraisal of the Klan which will appeal equally to all fair-minded men and women; reasons which seem to indicate that earlier judgments found against it were at least partly wrong, or have become wrong.

One is the quality of the people who are in the Klan or are joining it. They are not always, though sometimes, the best in the community, but they are usually the good, solid, middle-class citizens, the "back-bone of the nation." It is absurd to continue to believe that these people, so many and of such standing, are all criminal-minded; that they are any more likely to commit outrages than are the members of any other equal-sized body, such as the Presbyterian Church, or that they can or will become a menace to the country through any other cause than ignorance.

Confirming this quality of the Klan's present membership is the fact that even charges of Klan outrages have practically stopped. There are still reports in the papers concerning alleged outrages by Klan members happening some months ago, but I have found record of only three charged against the Klan since the early spring of 1923, and these have not been proved. It is possible to credit some of this to the increased influence of the Klan, which makes newspaper correspondents hesitate to report Klan outrage and papers hesitate to publish them. If this is so, it is rather startling testimony to the increased power of the Klan. It can not be wholly true, however, unless the entire newspaper world of the United States has sunk to an unspeakably low level, which is unthinkable, and even this would not explain silence by the many vigorously anti-Klan papers. It seems certain, then, that there is actually a tremendous improvement in this respect.

So it is clear that the opinion most of us formed two years ago, that the Klan was an attempt to gather the wild and lawless elements into a power, that it

3

was composed of gangs of night-riding hoodlums, probably criminal and certainly crazy, along with a scattering of feeble-minded people who had been hoodwinked—it is clear that this judgment is no longer correct, no matter how well-founded it seemed.

It is clear too that the Klan can no longer be dismissed as an unimportant though distressing outbreak of a few morons. Instead it has become a Great National Movement, with all the power and entitled to all the dignity and respect—yes, respect even if joined with fear and nervous ridicule—which belong to such movements. Whether for good or bad, whether insane or inspired, it must be studied, judged and dealt with on the basis of this growing importance.

And it is clear, finally, that since it has become such a movement quick action must be taken if it is to be diverted, controlled or stopped. Its power is very real; already there are strong influences getting into motion to use the power. If its leadership or programme is wrong the time when either can be changed will soon pass. When it has added the momentum of another million members or so it will be as difficult to divert from its course as a comet.

As to stopping it, destroying it, that seems unlikely for the present at least. The very fact of its power and growth to-day is proof enough that it has not been harmed by prosecution, persecution, ridicule, ignorant criticism or any other of the methods so far used. And whether the desire be to change, use,

4

fight or destroy it, the time is plainly here when nothing but facts will serve as ammunition.

It is, for example, pure folly any longer to attack it as lawless. It is true that lawlessness may be argued from its methods; true that lawless acts have been committed under cover of its hoods, true that a trusted official in the fall of 1923 killed a man in Atlanta. But when the great number of Klansmen is considered, with the fact that in many states there has never been an outrage that could even remotely be charged to them—and this in states where their strength is undoubted—and when it is further considered that of all the outrages attributed to the Klan not a dozen have been proved, fairness must admit that the charge falls as to actual conduct.

Since that is true, the charge of lawless intent gets nowhere. In almost all communities the Klan now has members who are known; they are not lawless either actually or in intention and such charges therefore seem absurd equally to them and to their non-Klan neighbors. Such charges simply are not believed and he who spreads them discredits himself.

The shoe in fact is now on the other foot; it is the legal officials who have become lawless, and the Klan which often suffers illegal persecution. The case of Oklahoma is the most flagrant. In that state Governor J. C. Walton overrode all constitutional restraints in his attempts to get at the Klan; imposed martial law without excuse, engaged gunmen who

5

made vigorous attempts to provoke the Klan to violence, suspended civil courts, and attempted by means of military courts-martial to fasten crimes upon the Klansmen. It was these excesses of Walton's which led to his being impeached and removed from office. Hundreds of minor officials all over the country have stretched their powers in the same way though to a less extent, in their efforts to suppress the Klan.

To give a single instance: A certain county judge ordered the arrest on sight of any Klan organizer, and when one was brought before him he shipped him out of the county. There was no trial, no charge could be proved, and the punishment is not one provided by any law. The judge justified his action on the theory that the Klan is in itself a menace to public peace and security. But since the law contemplates that action is required to constitute a crime, and since so far as is known no court has yet held that the Klan in and of itself is even a menace, much less criminal, it would seem that the legal fiction was stretched remarkably thin. At any rate other Klan organizers found the judge's action splendid propaganda for their cause, and the Klan now has more than 2,000 members in his county. It has been thus in many places. I get the impression that the Klan rather enjoys such attacks.

Perhaps that county will do as well as any other to illustrate the kind of men who are now joining the Klan. They are, if not the "best people," at least the next best. There are bankers, lawyers, doctors, probably a majority of the preachers, a handful of teachers, scores of small business men and hundreds upon hundreds of farmers.

But the Klan also reaches into higher places. In New York City three men may be mentioned as typical of its upper layer: a man very near the top of one of America's biggest manufacturing corporations, a doctor who is recognized as close to the head of his profession, and the owner of a powerful magazine. All, by the way, are active churchmen.

I learned in my investigations of one problem of Klan membership that has its elements of humor. The conscientious president of a large and highly respected fresh-water college is greatly disturbed in his mind whether to discharge the dozen or score of members of his faculty who have joined the organization. The Klan is watching him, rather hopefully, since such a raid would be splendid advertising and would also provide some very able martyrs for its propaganda bureau!

The total membership in the Klan to-day is, of course, a secret of the order. Klan officials refuse to give any figures. Others, whose information may or may not be accurate, say the total, including both men and women is now (January 30, 1924) about 6,000,-000. Detailed estimates, not by Klansmen, are that there are 500,000 each in Indiana and Ohio, 400,000 in Texas, more than 200,000 each in Oklahoma, Oregon, California and New York State, and from 50,000 to 200,000 each in Arkansas, Washington, Kansas, Missouri, Michigan, Illinois, Kentucky, West Virginia, Maryland, New Jersey, Louisiana, Mississippi, Alabama, Georgia, Florida and Tennessee. This would give a minimum total of 2,600,000 and a maximum of 5,000,000 which is not far from the Klan guess when allowance is made for scattered membership. My own opinion, based on estimates too complicated to bear repeating, is that the Klan strength is now just below 4,500,000. The larger figures are undoubtedly extravagant, for Klansmen are inclined to boast and politicians are frightened and subject to the complaint of "seeing things at night." But they will not be at all extravagant if the increase in Klan membership goes on at the present pace.

It is fairly amazing. I have spoken of the county where the judge's folly helped the Klan get 2,000 members. It took five men four weeks to do it, an average of a hundred a week for each man. This is probably a conservative average, for at one single meeting of which a report reached me—not from a Klansman—an organizer enlisted over five thousand recruits. This man held five meetings during that week. And there are—again the figures are approximate—some thousand Klan organizers at work. That would give a total "naturalization" of 100,000 a week! This agrees with an estimate I received from one of the leading Klan opponents. I believe it is approximately correct.

These people are all joining with a definite idea, for a definite purpose, and are willing to work under strict discipline to achieve that purpose. The result is a tremendously effective force. It is also tremendously active. Recent elections disclosed the fact that the Klan is politically entrenched in seven states: Oregon, Oklahoma, Texas, Arkansas, Indiana, Ohio and California. It is so powerful in a dozen others that no politician can by any possibility be driven to speak against it, at least not for publication. It is to be noted even in states which have passed anti-Klan laws that they are not being enforced, as with the celebrated Miller law in New York. Moreover, with few exceptions, the daily press has given over making attacks, gratuitous or otherwise. Everywhere there is the shadow of a power that those who depend on public good-will do not offend without compelling reasons.

Entrenched in seven states—great power in others— the Klan estimates that before the next election it can carry on intensive membership campaigns *in at least twenty-one more states!* The possible results of these campaigns may be guessed from the fact that similar ones gave it Ohio and Indiana in a few months, and are now giving it Michigan and Kentucky and Illinois.

So much for the power and importance of the Klan in our national life of to-day and to-morrow. It can hardly be exaggerated, but to be estimated correctly it

9

must be taken in connection with the fact that the history of the country has been filled with movements which were, in a general way, quite similar. Time after time there have broken out organized efforts to restrict the power of alien-born and particularly of Roman Catholic citizens. Each has raged with bitterness, each has gained some headway, and each has vanished suddenly.

It was surprising to find out how little the heads of the Klan knew of this historic background. To them the movement is a natural outgrowth of present conditions, almost unique, facing problems the nation has never faced before. Yet it may almost be said that such a movement is a normal accompaniment of any such state of mental and moral unrest as America is now undergoing. From these previous agitations, in spite of certain differences between them and the Klan idea which will be detailed in later chapters, much may be learned as to the probable strength, probable results and the equally probable prompt disappearance of Ku Kluxism.

These movements have been dubbed "nativistic" by certain historians and political writers. The word has rather a horrendous sound and is undoubtedly intended to express contempt. Yet the fundamental idea on which all these movements agree is at least one on which opinion may honestly be divided. It is merely this: That native-born citizens, trained in the national schools, sons and heirs of the men who built up the nation, are on the whole better interpreters of national thought and purposes, and hence better fitted to rule the country, than are people of alien blood, tradition and training, whom those natives have admitted to a share in their advantages.

This idea seems hardly criminal. It may fairly be called illiberal, with whatever stigma that adjective implies in view of the recent demonstration that liberalism may wander far from common-sense patriotism.

The first, then, of the "nativistic" movements, came in the very early years of the republic. The Federalists wished a firm central government; the newly arrived preferred a weak one. So the Federalists made the alien vote an issue and in 1795 raised the term of naturalization to fourteen years. The Democratic-Republicans, under Jefferson, restored the term to five years in 1802 and grew powerful on the alien vote—as other political parties have done several times since. The issue was kept alive till it disappeared in the War of 1812.

It revived again in New York City in 1835 when the alien voters definitely banded together to control the city, parading with banners which read: "Americans must not rule us!" The response of the Americans was instant. They rallied under the leadership of prominent men, of whom Samuel F. B. Morse, inventor of the telegraph, was one of the best known. He wrote the famous "Brutus" letters, charging that there was an alien, Roman Catholic conspiracy to seize control of America. He attacked the "compact and clannish body of immigrants, avid of office and openly allying themselves as foreigners against the nation." The movement resulted in practically driving foreigners from office in New York City, spread to Boston and Philadelphia where there were riots, and then slumbered.

The next outbreak was in 1843 when the Democrats again carried New York City and gave the majority of offices to foreigners. Again the alien issue won control, and again there were riots and bloodshed and much bitterness. One notable outrage was the looting and burning of a nunnery. Having accomplished its immediate purposes it again died.

But the alien issue became a tremendous one in 1853. The big immigration from Ireland following the famine of 1847, and from the Continent as a result of the abortive revolutionary movements in 1848–50 swamped the American voters. This resulted in the formation of "The Sons of 1776, or the Order of the Star Spangled Banner," the lower lodges of which were pledged to vote for none but native Protestants— there was no negro question then—and the higher orders, to force foreigners and Catholics out of all public service. The members were instructed to answer "I don't know" to all questions, and so got the name of "Know-nothings."

My own boyhood study of history left me with the

THE GIANT IN THE WHITE HOOD

impression that the Know-nothings were a queer, obscure and rather disreputable lot, without any particular influence. This is far from the fact. They nearly got control of the country. Operating at first by endorsing selected candidates—as the Anti-Saloon League has done and the Ku Klux Klan is doing now —they upset all political calculations in 1853 and 1854. In 1855 their success went to their heads and they came into the open as the American Party. This, as events proved, was a fatal mistake, but it won great immediate success. In that year they carried nine states, and narrowly missed six others; the next year they had eight governors and fourteen legislatures. A side-light on their standing and membership is the fact that they elected twenty-four ministers to the Massachusetts legislature. Their strength was chiefly in New England and the South, though they showed sporadic power in all parts of the country.

But the movement died fast. Being a political party it was forced to take a stand on the burning question of slavery, tried to straddle, lost everything but the border states in '58, and by '60, after a vain effort to avert the war, had almost vanished. Nathaniel Wright Stephenson, the historian, says that "about the only definite thing it accomplished was the binding together of the different racial stocks," but its temporary achievement was much greater. It did, for the time, clean up much local political corruption and drive from office many foreigners and Roman Catholics.

Both groups remembered Know-nothingism after its power was gone, and their efforts, combined with its pusillanimous record on slavery, covered it with obloquy. Its members hunted cover, and it has never had a friendly historian. Perhaps it did not deserve one, for its propaganda was based on absurdly lurid stories about the Catholic Church, and was from first to last little but an appeal to prejudice, lacking the dignity of the Morse movement. But it very nearly won complete success.

Following the Civil War there was one other outbreak, the American Protective Association, but it fell under the disrepute left over from the Know-nothings, and though it once claimed two million members, never achieved any power. The last flicker from it was the Rev. Dr. Burchard's famous "Rum, Romanism and Rebellion," which contributed to the defeat of Blaine for the presidency. That debacle convinced politicians once for all that the anti-alien, anti-Catholic agitation was too dangerous to monkey with.

So, in spite of all the talk of unfit immigration, unassimilated aliens, hyphen-ism, and perversion of Americanism which has been heard in the last few years, the Ku Klux Klan is the first to dare raise the fundamental issue openly once more. History, as well as the Klan's own success, shows how powerful an appeal that issue may have. And the Klan has not yet made, and its leaders declare that it will not make, the mistakes which wrecked the Know-nothings. It is evident that the possibilities in such a situation confuse the imagination.

It is evident, too, that an organization which has grown as fast as the Klan has grown and has won such support from so solid a class of citizens—all in the face of the bitterest opposition, possesses enormous vitality. There is a deeper reason for its existence than a desire to masquerade in white hoods, or even to go night-riding and reform the neighbors with a black-snake whip. Such a growth, in itself, proves that the movement has an appeal to some deep-rooted sentiment, instinct, prejudice, condition or whatever you care to call it, but something wide-spread, fundamental and very much alive.

This book is an attempt to report with as little bias as possible all the facts that can be learned in a very confused and fast changing situation, about the Ku Klux Klan, its purposes and why so many citizens indorse them, its methods and the reasons for their success, the type of individuals who are joining and why, the good results it may accomplish and the undoubted dangers it brings in its train. The book therefore is neither a crusade, an exposure, nor a defense; its only purpose is to set forth the information needed for sound judgment on a complicated and highly explosive condition, a condition which has grown needlessly obscure because much that has taken place in recent years has been passed over in silence, and much more has been misrepresented.

THE CHALLENGE OF THE KLAN

If there is bias in this report, it works both ways. First, is the conviction that four million American citizens, the great majority of whom lead decent, god-fearing, law-abiding and useful lives, can not be condemned offhand as either idiots or criminals. A movement that has won their support, even though it may seem both ridiculous and wrong-headed, must have behind it some motives, impulses and purposes of very considerable appeal and apparent soundness. And even if they are utterly wrong, the very fact that they exist is of the utmost importance, because of the effect they may have on our national life.

The second bias, if it is that, is a belief that because of the first bias there must be a new judgment on the Klan which must be based on neither denunciation of occasional crimes, nor on vague indignation against mysterious methods and half-understood purposes. Instead there must be a careful estimate of the patriotic values or dangers of the motives and ideals professed, based on a determination whether the Klan does actually further those motives and ideals, and finally on a decision whether its methods and propaganda contain a menace greater than lies within the evils it assumes to cure. This book is written in the further belief that only in the light of a judgment so formed can current affairs be properly understood, and that such a judgment is necessary even for effective dealing with the Klan or resistance to it.

CHAPTER II

THE GIANT CLEARS FOR ACTION

THE Ku Klux Klan to-day is a very different organization from that of two years ago, when it was investigated by Congress and found guilty by public opinion of serious crimes. This is the first fact about it that strikes an inquirer. It is different in leadership, in personnel, in purposes and in methods. Its leaders, to be sure, declare that the difference is merely a change of emphasis, but this seems to be nothing more than an attempt on their part to hold the previously acquired membership and maintain the strength that comes from tradition. But the fact is, there has been a deliberate overhauling. In it, whatever of the old Klan seemed useful has been kept, but there have been important rejections and much that is new has been added.

These changes are carefully calculated by a shrewd and understanding mind. The new leaders recognized that the position of the Klan and its reputation were fatally weak. They had large ambitions, and set about to make the Klan at once less easy to attack and far more effective in its appeal to the average decent citizen. They developed new strategy, new tactics. In short, the Giant in the White Hood sought to clear the decks for action. How well he succeeded is partly proved by the growth that followed.

The first result is that the Klan to-day is far less subject to the kind of criticism which has a direct, simple, emotional appeal, than it was two years ago. The Giant is wearing better armor. There is less and less truth in the old indictments for violence and graft; also they are less and less effective with those who know the new Klan—and it is taking pains to be known by those whom it wishes to enlist. It is putting out a strong propaganda, and with much success, to show that it is not in any way a champion or defender of lawlessness. Behind the propaganda is an effort to make sure that no such showing can ever again be made against it as was made before the Congressional Investigating Committee.

Moreover, it has adopted a rather different objective; at least a very different definition of its old objectives. Though it has kept the fundamental idea unchanged—"America for Americans"—it has attempted to formulate a propaganda which does not appeal to hate nor stimulate violent prejudices except as the idea itself does so, and a programme which is broader, more definite, and that offers opportunity for lawful and satisfying action. It has tried thus to hold

18

THE GIANT CLEARS FOR ACTION

the most effective of its old appeals, to widen their scope and to make them proof against easy attack. Finally, it is using very different methods. In place of the black-snake whip and physical terrorism it has adopted new weapons far more subtle and more dangerous and far less open to simple or obvious criticisms. Though it has stopped night-riding it has not abandoned terrorism, but has put it on a mental, social and economic basis. It has added the most effective methods of a political minority and other methods even more effective, which are not exactly new in American politics, but have never been employed by so tremendous an organization. One may easily disapprove these methods, but they are not illegal and they are not peculiar to the Klan except in that it uses them more scientifically and effectively than do others.

In general, it may be said that the most important result of these reforms has been to change the Ku Klux Klan from an organization which could have an appeal only in the South to one with a very broad national outlook and interest. Each of the more important changes has modified the Klan's purposes or methods to make them less open to the criticism of the average decent man north of the Mason and Dixon line. It is probable that the Klan could never have made its great expansion in the northern and midwestern states if it had not rid itself of the incubus incurred by night-riding and similar outrages.

19

THE CHALLENGE OF THE KLAN

This reform of the Giant began shortly after the exposures already referred to. It was so far completed by 1923 that the new Klan was ready to launch the campaign which has had such success. The reformation has been carried further now, and the Klan is about prepared to lay its case before the bar of public opinion. Its leaders have full confidence that, at least, no serious objections to its programme can be found by the great majority of decent people, and that there is ample justification for its methods in the emergency they believe to exist.

The first step in the reform was the obvious one, to remove the opportunity for attacks based on reputation for graft, for fomenting disorder and violence, for being a menace to law and order, and for attempting to substitute itself for the Government. The Klan considers that this has been done.

"I will say to you this," said H. W. Evans, the Imperial Wizard, when I asked him how much success his reform campaign had achieved: "As much progress has been made as it seems to me could have been expected within the short time since the change in control of the Klan took place. The Klan is now, on the whole, as entirely free from those evils in personnel as can be expected, so far as we have definitely ascertained. Naturally, such failures on the part of the members are continually occurring—a situation which is perfectly sound may become unsound within a few weeks or a month—but whenever such a situation arises it is corrected as soon as the facts are learned.

"Failures on the part of individuals to live up to convictions and teachings are always betrayals of trust. Klansmen are not free from them, but we have arrived at the point where the Klan recognizes that such actions are in direct conflict with its doctrine and oath.

"The Klan, as a whole, has heartily supported all corrective measures, making reform easier and more expeditious."

This statement, which admits the previous charges against the Klan and the fact of the house-cleaning, and which admits also that the organization is not yet perfect, is quite typical of Dr. Evans. Before taking up the story of what he has done to the Klan let us stop for a moment to look at the man himself. His position as Wizard makes him one of the most influential men in America to-day. On him, too, depends largely whether the achievements of the Klan be good or bad. As one of the highest grade men I know—an ardent Klansman—said to me—"If the Klan should be perverted it would be the most dangerous body that ever existed. It would do incalculable harm." Dr. Evans, to-day, would be the man who would have to pervert it.

Hiram Wesley Evans, then, is a man in the middle forties; of middle height, too, and tending toward flesh. He is smooth-shaved, round-headed and rather round-faced, with the slightly prominent eyes so often found in politicians. His gaze is clear and direct; his mouth firm, though full, his hands supple and active, but without much refinement. He dresses carefully. His sense of humor is direct and blunt but not coarse.

He is a Texan born, a dentist by profession, an active member of the Christian or Disciples' Church, and a Thirty-second Degree Mason, as are many of the Klan leaders. He is a natural orator and speaks with the softness and peculiarities of the South and with something of the tang and rotundity of the old-fashioned political oratory. He gives the impression of tremendous activity, backed by great force. His address would lack appeal to an "intellectual" audience; it is extremely effective with "common people."

I was told by one of his intimates, before I saw him, that he was not a great man, that the strength of the Klan was in its ideas rather than in its leaders, but that he was decidedly efficient. My contacts with him confirmed this estimate. He seemed an excellent organizer, promoter and administrator—qualities not always combined—but not strongly original or imaginative. He appeared most remarkable for practical common sense, he has an undoubted instinct for politics, he understands the average citizen intuitively, rather than by study. He was with me, though not always for publication, briskly honest so far as I have been able to check up on his statements. He is direct in thought, though verbose in statement; he is not

22

highly educated nor highly cultured, his thoughts and feelings are those of the commonalty rather than of the intellectuals. He seemed sincere, and as honest and sound as a good apple; he is under heavy pressure and strong temptations, but all the indications are that he has so far resisted both and that his selling price—since every man must have a price—is very high. He described himself to me as "the most average man in America," and that can not be improved as a thumbnail sketch.

The story of what Dr. Evans has done to the Klan and for it came mostly from other people. He said little about it, except as to results, and when he did speak he was careful always to identify himself with the mass, to appear no more than their leader and spokesman. Yet the evidence is that he has almost single-handed taken control of the organization and changed it to his purpose. There seems to be no doubt that this purpose includes personal ambitions for power, probably for position and possibly for wealth, but there seems also no doubt that he expects to achieve these through carrying the Klan to power and success, and that he is too canny to risk losing the great triumph for the sake of any minor self-gratifications.

There is no need to devote much space to the early history of the Klan. It was founded in 1915 in Atlanta by Col. W. J. Simmons, a preacher, dreamer and —even according to his enemies—something of an idealist, however warped. His imagination had been

THE CHALLENGE OF THE KLAN

stirred by outbreaks of race and religious prejudices in Georgia and by the hyphenism of the war; he felt that the law was failing to protect the rights of America as well as of Americans against organized conspirators, and he set out on a campaign of correction. He founded his Order along the lines of the Ku Klux Klan of reconstruction days, which many believe saved the South from negroes and carpet-baggers. He won some immediate success in enlisting members through his appeal to the tradition of honor in which the South holds the Klan of the 'sixties.

Whether he intended it or not, the tradition of the lawless methods of the 'sixties was also carried over, though the new Klan had none of the justifications for violence which the old could claim. Many men take easily to night-riding and a good many took the cover of the new Klan to indulge this passion. The result was to bring the Klan into immediate disrepute throughout the country. The story of the outrages committed under the White Hoods at that time is too well-known to need repetition here.

Colonel Simmons, as has been said, is a dreamer; he is nothing of an organizer. The Klan grew very slowly, so presently he made a contract with Edward Young Clark, who had been highly successful as an organizer of drives, by which Clark was to get 80 per cent. of the initiation fees of $10.00 each. Clark had considerable success, though his organizers are accused of appealing to the worst motives and prejudices, and

24

so did the Klan great harm. After paying them, Clark's profits were considerable; he is said to have made as high as $40,000 a month. Charges of graft and corruption naturally resulted.

The Congressional inquiry, the exposure in newspapers and magazines and the storm of condemnation which followed, nearly broke Simmons' heart. He understood it but little and although the Klan was so organized that he could never have been ousted, he resigned, undoubtedly under pressure from the Evans crowd.

"Texas was the star Klan state and we came to the meeting all ready to go ahead and do something," one of them said. "But when we got there we found the Klan was not going anywhere or aiming to do anything, so we got busy, and Simmons done saw the need of a change."

"There was a bunch of us in Indiana who saw that something had to be done if the Klan was really going to amount to anything," an Indianapolis man told me. "We started an agitation that got the better men throughout the Klan together and we managed to show Simmons that he was not the man for the place."

I am unable to pass judgment between the rival claimants. My own impression is that the reforms came as a spontaneous movement in which all the better men of the Klan joined, and that they were very largely due to the condemnation which fell upon the

Klan as the result of the exposures in the Congressional investigation.

About the first thing Evans did was to cancel Clark's contract. This precipitated a fight which is still going on. Simmons stood by his friends, backed by the Atlanta Klan. The Evans group revoked its charter. Although the fight is hot in Atlanta, I have found little evidence of it elsewhere. It is certainly having little effect on the power or growth of the Klan under Evans, and does not seem to threaten his control. Its chief importance has been to bring out some facts about the Klan, and to show how complete is the divergence between the old Klansmen and the new. Colonel Simmons declares that Evans has utterly betrayed the Klan and perverted its ideals.

The fight is receiving newspaper notice apparently out of all proportion to its actual importance. There are, in many parts of the country, a small number of Klans that have never received charters from the National organization and most of which are supporting Clark and Simmons. There are also probably a few members of the regular Klan, mostly in the South, who have leanings in this direction. Mr. Clark's attack on the Klan and his offer to President Coolidge to help him in exposing it, have made Klansmen regard him as a traitor. They resulted in the banishment of both himself and Colonel Simmons, who was supporting him. When it is remembered that Clark's conduct drew a large part of the criticism in previous investigations and that the attack on the old Klan centered upon him, it will be seen how little likelihood there is that he will win any great success in his present attempt to undermine Evans. The reforms he suggests are undoubtedly desirable in many ways, but the fact that it is he who has suggested them will make it very difficult to get them considered on their merits.

One result of the Evans régime was at once apparent; big personal profits were stopped. Clark had built a splendid home in Atlanta. Evans lived for a year in a $65.00 a month flat. When Evans took charge the Klan treasury held only about $100,000. The finances, by the way, are under the complete control of the Wizard. By July 31, 1923, according to Court audit, the treasury held assets of $1,087,273 and liabilities of $1,705 (balance $1,085,568) as against assets of $403,173 and liabilities of $247,227 (balance $155,946) a year before. Dr. Evans and his friends feel that they are pretty well clear of the charge of graft.

This matter being attended to, Dr. Evans took up the question of lawlessness. His practical mind saw clearly that it not only accomplished nothing, but that it aroused opposition, gave enemies of the Klan their best ground for attack, and emphatically blocked all possibility of carrying the Klan into the northern states or among the better classes anywhere and so of making it a real power. This is apart from his personal views on the morals of violence. On these he spoke to me as strongly as any enemy of the Klan ever has spoken or ever could speak.

"Violent methods are never justifiable," he declared, "not even when the ordinary agencies of law have broken down. Violent measures should never be used, and corrective measures applied to individuals by any persons except duly elected law officers are never right. Neither of them is practised and neither is permitted by the Klan."

At first he gave his attention to specific instances of violence, often going to places where trouble was brewing. One story is told of a town in which the anti-Klan forces had organized to break up a Klavern (Klan assembly). Evans managed to get to the meeting but after it had assembled, and found some hundred and forty men, all armed to the teeth ready to go forth to battle. Around the house was a mob, not well-organized but dangerous. Evans took his stand before the door and for hours argued with his followers. In the end he induced them to leave their arms in the building and go out defenseless. Some were wounded, many were mauled, but not one struck a blow. By this and similar means he tried to establish the idea that a Klansman must not use violence.

But he soon found that this was not enough, and so made an open and direct fight inside the Order. This culminated in a meeting of the Grand Dragons (state heads) with minor officials at Asheville last July. At this meeting he not only defined the new purposes and methods he had been perfecting, as will be told in a later chapter, but laid down the law on the subject of violence. In closing his address he said:

"We have not been appointed by Almighty God or any Imperial Wizard to go out meddling in other peoples' business. Our duty is to get behind the constituted officers of the law, as every one of you has sworn to do. Let's get a National Law enforcement programme—let's fix it so people will have to go to the penitentiaries for violating law. You can not enforce laws in the form of a super-government trying to force your will or your government on the law of the land. The first time one of your Klansmen violates the law, thus breaking his obligation, thus doing a thing in direct conflict with that for which we stand, let us administer on him as Klansmen for breaking his obligation. Let us then get them outside the Klan and let the judge and jury and the penitentiary take care of them. When we do this, the thing will fade like the morning dew.

"The Wizard is not responsible for any violation. I am going to tell you now: go home and do your duty and the first time you have a bunch of Klansmen that break a law, do not get behind them. Put your influence with the constituted officers of the law, and go with the law and act through the law and thus once and for all and eternally end this accusation."

This, mind you, was to Klansmen alone, and not a public statement. Dr. Evans may have intended to make it public later, but the Klansmen gathered could not know that. A further light on his orders is thrown by the following quotation from a speech, at the same meeting, by Clay Jewett, one of his strong supporters and intimate friends, whom he had recently chosen to reform the Klan in Oklahoma.

"You are all well acquainted with the plan of the organization of Klankraft, the method of administration and the many radical changes of operation since the Order was originally conceived and promulgated. One of the great faults in the organization of the Klans throughout the various realms (states) now established, was the class of propaganda which the representatives first engaged in this work saw fit to promulgate.

"In their zeal to establish a record and in order to awaken a certain interest in the hearts of men with whom they came in contact, they, in many instances, secured the attention of those men by stories pertaining to the operation of the old Klan in 1866, wherein the whip was the chief instrument of persuasion. In relating such stories, these organizers did not perhaps make a statement to the effect that this was the purpose of the organization, nevertheless, they would leave the impression in the minds of the newly created Klansmen that it was one of the features of the organization. Frequently such stories merely encouraged the idea that we should, by right, take the law in our own hands in these cases where apparently the law did not function or properly handle the offender. Nothing could be more erroneous than this idea, and organizers who resort to such practises have done a great deal of harm to the growth of our Order."

Dr. Evans soon succeeded in getting at the head of the Klan in various states men who supported this campaign. One such is Gen. Nathan Bedford Forrest, Grand Dragon of Georgia, and son of the famous Confederate General who was head of the Klan of '66. Gen. Forrest is an unusually high type of man, strong and clean, and he has made an open fight. His "realm" was one of the worst, since it was the first organized under the old methods. His record, however, is typical of several other southern Grand Dragons.

General Forrest told me with some bitterness how people in Georgia were continually calling on the Klan to redress their personal grievances by either threatening or beating up some neighbor. He mentioned at least three cases where women had applied to the Klan to perform lynchings for them, and said that he got on an average over twenty letters a week of this kind.

"Of course, we do nothing with them," he said, "except to turn them over to the regular law officers in the neighborhood. Whatever may have been the case in the earlier days of the Klan, the organization has now been made to realize that its officials and the Klan itself do not countenance or support lawlessness or private justice of any kind. There are possibly

31

individual Klansmen who still try to do this, but we are doing our best to suppress it. Our efforts toward law enforcement are limited entirely to giving information to officials or bringing influence to bear upon them. If we find that they fail in their duty, then we tell the local Klansmen the facts and let them take action in the next election."

He admitted that there were some cases in which people had used the Klan regalia to cover crimes, and fewer cases in which Klansmen themselves had broken the law, always without sanction of the Klan. Wherever this is suspected to have occurred, the local Klan is under orders to help bring the offenders to justice. Gen. Forrest, as Grand Dragon, has offered a reward of $1,500 for the conviction of any Klansman, and in Macon, where some night-riders were on trial and Klansmen were suspected, he sent detectives to work under the sheriff. Men were finally brought to trial on their evidence, and he had a statement made in Court that the Klan did not endorse, support or protect the men. In at least four cases where local Klans have misbehaved, he has revoked their charters, and given his evidence against them to the courts.

He has got results. "The Klan used to be made up of riff-raff—not criminals, but rowdies and low-class folks," one of the best known men in Georgia told me, and others agreed. "Now it is getting the reputation of being a decent organization and a lot of much better men are joining it. This is mostly since violence has been stopped. There has been very little for some time."

The final measure taken to stop violence is, perhaps, a good test of the sincerity of the reform. In many states no member is now permitted to take his regalia from the Klavern without permission. All hoods and robes are checked with a doorkeeper, and are never in possession of a Klansman except for official business. This measure destroys the chief excuse of the Klan in case of outrages—the plea that the regalia was used without permission.

There is accumulating evidence that the Klan is more and more letting the use of the hood drop into the background, although a new arrangement made by Dr. Evans has resulted in bringing the price down to five dollars. At present only about one-third of the members actually own hoods and robes. The rules of the order are that every man must have them, so the suspicion is justified that the officials are allowing to drop into disuse a custom which they can not officially change.

In every place where I investigated, or from which I have reports, this reform of the Klan has been made plain to every member and is insisted upon in all propaganda. Thus, officially, at least, the Klan has cleared its skirts. The extent to which the change has been accepted by the members is another matter, which will be taken up later. But since there are now so few reports of Klan violence, it seems clear that until new

33

evidence appears the new orders must be accepted as a real position, fairly well maintained. So far as the leaders are concerned or can make their efforts effective, the Klan does not take the law into its own hands, nor permit its members to do so.

Opponents of the Klan naturally deny the sincerity of this reform. They charge that it was forced by the exposures and the prospect of internal disruption, that it is purely hypocritical, a matter of tactics adopted for the expediency of the moment which will be abandoned whenever some new expediency dictates.

There is, of course, no means at the disposal of a reporter to determine men's motives. I put the question to a leading Klansman.

"I can't prove to you that it isn't so," he smiled. "But I will point out two things. First: the Klan is absolutely committed, inside and out. If it fails to live up to the reform it will be damned much more completely than before. Second: the great influx of members has come since the law and order programme was made clear. They prove that this programme is good policy. The Klan will not be foolish enough to change. Moreover, the new members agree with this principle, they now constitute a majority, and they will see that it is lived up to."

My own opinion on the reform, for whatever it is worth, is that the change is sincere enough for all practical purposes. I believe that Dr. Evans is perfectly honest in his detestation of violence, and that

34

both he and a majority of his followers are convinced also that purely as a matter of policy, violence and physical terrorism do not pay. Therefore, I think their abandonment of them is sincere and as complete as they can make it. Since, for practical social purposes, hypocrisy well lived up to is as useful as sincerity, this seems a sufficient answer to the question.

This reform, then, is the first and most important step of the Klan in preparing for its great campaign. So far as it is successful and gains credence it will protect the movement from the charges which have been the only basis for most of the attacks on it. Dr. Evans reasons with some soundness that the whole attack will fail if those charges become untenable. Certainly, enemies of the Klan would be forced to find new grounds for attack—not a great hardship in view of the failure of their efforts to prevent the growth of the Klan so far. Certainly, also, new attacks would have to be based on the new ideals, programme and methods of the Klan, even though such attacks would be more difficult than the old, calling for argument and intelligence rather than for simple condemnation.

CHAPTER III

WHEN Col. Simmons in 1915 formed his new Ku Klux Klan along the lines of the Klan of 1866 he inevitably took over in one bundle not only the form but much of the tradition and of the ideas of terrorism, violence and defiance of government on which the older organization was built. They may not have been part of his intentions; they simply were there, whatever he or any one else said or did. So, although the Klan as Dr. Evans is now handling it is considerably changed and far less open to obvious criticism, it remains the same in many essentials.

Not all people will believe that these inherent qualities are wholly evil and dangerous. Some actually believe in them; some will hold that, even if objectionable, they are necessary; some that the good they may accomplish outweighs the danger. But to an outsider they certainly appear, at least on the surface, to be not only highly menacing but also sharply inconsistent with the purpose and ideals which the Klan professes. They make it easy to believe the Klan is utterly hypo-

36

critical. But, giving Dr. Evans and his associates
every credit for idealism and sincere patriotism, these
things still seem so fundamental that his whole effort
must come under suspicion of being an attempt to
grow figs on a thistle.

I say "on the surface" because Klan leaders, though
admitting in some degree the danger and in larger
degree the risk of misunderstanding, deny that these
things are what they seem, or that any of them are as
dangerous as they appear. These explanations and
defenses will be given in proper place; however convincing they may or may not be, it is certain that
before taking up the purposes, protestations, strategy
and tactics of the Klan, the organization which is behind them should be studied carefully.

Most important, because it permeates the whole
structure and of necessity colors all first impressions
of the Klan for members as well as outsiders, is the
tradition of the Klan of the 'sixties. That body,
springing out of the desperate needs of reconstruction
days, when what government there was had fallen
into the hands of ignorant and often vicious negroes,
led by northerners so depraved that "carpet-bagger"
has become a name of supreme contempt, that body
did heroic work. It enabled the few and politically
powerless survivors of the armies of the Confederacy
to check terrific lawlessness, prevent hideous crimes,
and save the remnants of their civilization. It has
left a tradition of high honor through the South.

Equally, because of the blazing hatred and misunderstandings of those days, it was condemned through the North. Its justification is not in question here.

The important fact about it is that *it was an organization of terror.* Its regalia, its secrecy, its oaths, the titles of its officers, the form of the organization itself, were all intended to paralyze with fright those against whom it was directed, black or white. Many of them actually believed in wizards, ghosts and dragons. The swift blow in the night, the invisible power which struck, the ghastly regalia—all combined to create overpowering horror. The organization, too, was at war with the obnoxious governments that then existed, and was adapted to defy and evade them. It was a real "invisible empire," a true super-government. It was militant, autocratic, irresponsible.

And it was diabolically effective. It was so effective that its creators destroyed it, carefully and completely. As soon as the gravest disorder had passed, and long before normal conditions had been restored, the leaders, who were among the best men in the South, decided that the dangers were so great, the inherent evils so menacing, and the impossibility of control so manifest, that it could not be allowed to live. In 1869 Gen. Nathan Sedford Forrest, the Grand Wizard, issued an order which dissolved it almost in a night.

This is the organization which the new Klan has imitated and of which it claims to be the heir; this the tradition it took over. It has added much to the formulas and purposes of the older Order, which drew no line against Catholics, Jews or alien born. But since it claims spiritual heirship, the burden of proof is on it if it is to escape condemnation for reviving in quiet times all the menaces which the old Klan used under hideous emergency, and quickly abandoned.

The new Klan, it is true, has in it some of the men who were members of the old, and their sons. But it also has some of both among its opponents. A son of one of Lee's officers condemns it as follows:

"This outfit is a plain impostor. There's nothing of the old Klan about it but the name and nonsense. Maybe it's got some of the riff-raff who made the trouble that caused the old Klan to disband—I don't know. But no true member of the old Klan and no true southerner can draw the lines that this gang does. The old Klan had Catholics in it, and Jews. No man who loves the memory of the Confederacy is going to join a crowd that would bar out Judah P. Benjamin, General Beauregard and a dozen like them. No, sir!"

First of the characteristics of the old Klan which mark the new and which must be judged in the light of the old tradition, is the mask and all it implies of secrecy and terrorism. This is, to begin with, a secrecy different from that of other fraternities. They protect their ritual and purposes, as the Klan does; the Klan hides its members as well.

The efforts Dr. Evans has made to remove the

threat of physical terrorism from the Klan regalia have already been described. But even if those efforts should become completely successful this form of secrecy is open to very grave objections. I know of several high-grade men, now fighting the Klan, who have told me that they would join it if, as one of them put it, they could "wear a Klan button."

One of the obvious dangers is the possibility of the perversion of the Order. Behind its veil it could be swung swiftly from one objective to another; it could be used in whole or in part—without the knowledge of better-class members—for purposes to which they were bitterly opposed, but which they would aid through the very fact of their membership.

More serious is the fact that it makes the Klan utterly irresponsible except to the consciences of Klansmen. It can strike in the dark as the old Klan struck—and this covers much more than mere physical violence—and leave no clue. Its actions, whether good or bad, may sometimes be suspected, but can seldom be proved. Its officers are in the open, to be sure, but they can easily deny or claim what they wish. Thus the Klan is almost perfectly un-get-at-able either by the public or the Government.

"The Government made every effort to suppress the Klan," writes General Forrest of reconstruction days, "but it was utterly powerless." The new Klan is similarly organized. If it has the man-power and the desire it can become in very fact an "invisible empire."

OLD EVILS IN THE NEW KLAN

But most serious of all is the terrorism, the implied threat of the mask. It is not enough for the Klan to deny that it intends any such threat, not enough, even, for it to avoid violence. The very existence of a masked organization makes it possible for any group of adventurers or criminals to act under Klan disguise and often to gain something in safety thereby. The essential fact is that the mask, in its very nature, is a threat. It was devised by the old Klan for that purpose. Public opinion so holds it; holds that to have bodies of masked men wandering around in disguise is in itself a threat against peace and law. At least one jury—in Amarillo, Texas—has held that the wearing of Klan regalia in public is a menace in and by itself, and on that verdict a man was sentenced to two years in the penitentiary.

A second class of objections to the Klan springs from the form of the organization; not merely the grotesque and ludicrous names and language, but the method of control, the oaths and obligations and the great danger that members will put a vicious interpretation on them and on the Klan symbolism. All these are all wide open to attack.

To any one unfamiliar with the extravagances of secret societies, and even to some who are familiar, the nomenclature of the Klan offers a broad target. By official title its officers are an array of mythological monsters and nightmare absurdities. For example, the proclamation of the Klan constitution reads:

THE CHALLENGE OF THE KLAN

"To all Genii, Grand Dragons and Hydras, Great Titans and Furies, Giants, Exalted Cyclops and Terrors, and to all citizens of the Invisible Empire," etc.

The organization and the meanings of these fabulous titles are as follows:

The nominal head of the organization is the Emperor, who has no real power, but has authority over ritual, regalia, titles, etc. The actual executive head is the Imperial Wizard. Gathered around him are a Kloncilium, composed of the following "genii," all "imperial": Klaliff, Klazik—vice-presidents; Klokard —lecturer; Kludd—chaplain; Kligrapp—secretary; Klabee—treasurer; Kladd—conductor; Klarogo—inner guard; Klexter—outer guard; Klonsel—counsel; Night-hawk—courier; and four Klokann—auditors and advisers. The legislative body of the Klan is a Klonvocation.

Each state is a realm, headed by a Grand Dragon, having a council similarly named except that the members are "grand" instead of "imperial," and are the "Hydras." A "province," usually a county, is headed by a Great Titan, its council members are "great" and are "Furies"; the individual Klan, occupying a. Klanton, is headed by an Exalted Cyclops, and the members of his council are "Terrors." A "Giant" is an ex-officer, with some appropriate adjective; thus an ex-wizard is an Imperial Giant, and an ex-cyclops merely a Klan Giant. A Kleagle, now fairly well-known, is an organizer.

OLD EVILS IN THE NEW KLAN

There is much of this sort of stuff, too much to be worth detailing, as it is all along the same lines, except perhaps the Klan Kalendar, now in its 58th year. In it the days of the week are in order, "dark, deadly, dismal, doleful, desolate, dreadful and desperate," the weeks are "woeful, weeping, wailing, wonderful and weird," and the months "bloody, gloomy, hideous, fearful, furious, alarming, terrible, horrible, mournful, sorrowful, frightful and appalling." Thus the revised Klan Constitution—I have not learned why it is not a Klonstiklution—was officially proclaimed on November 29, 1922, or "on the Doleful Day of the Weird Week of the Terrible Month of the year of the Klan LVI."

In view of all the nomenclature, this seems a fitting date!

All this, however, is not merely funny. A Klansman must take these names more or less seriously; they have a meaning. However they are now interpreted—I have learned nothing about the ritualistic symbolism of the Order—they carry on their face the mark of the terroristic purposes of the old Klan. So, too, do the insignia; the fiery cross, originally used to call the Scottish clans to arms and a symbol of alarm from time immemorial; the crossed swords which lie upon the Bible before its shrines; the robed and mounted horseman; the dragon on the ensign with arrowheads for tongue and tail, and all the rest.

So, too, does much of the language of the oaths and

the Constitution. The very name of "Invisible Empire" has a sinister meaning in common speech and thought; "Imperial Authority" to which the Klansman swears allegiance, the titles of his officers, his oath to enforce the law himself as well as to aid officers of the law—all these things combine to give to the outsider an impression, however they may be explained, of a basic "complex" of militant activity hardly consistent with complete obedience to the Nation's laws.

Since these documents are of such importance in defining the purposes and showing the organized power of the Klan, it is worth while to give considerable attention to them. The most important is undoubtedly the Oath of Allegiance. In the text of the Oath, as printed for Klan use, there are asterisks in place of the name of the Klan and of certain other identifying words. In the following text these have been filled in and the directions as to the action of the initiate have been omitted:

OATH OF ALLEGIANCE—KU KLUX KLAN

SECTION I—*Obedience*

"I, ———, in the presence of God and Man most solemnly pledge, promise and swear unconditionally, that I will faithfully obey the constitution and laws and will willingly conform to all regulations, usages

44

and requirements of the Knights of the Ku Klux Klan which do now exist or which may hereafter be enacted, and will render at all times loyal respect and steadfast support to the Imperial Authority of the same, and will heartily heed all official mandates, decrees, edicts, rulings and instructions of the Imperial Wizard thereof. I will yield prompt response to all summonses, I having knowledge of same, Providence alone preventing.

Section II—*Secrecy*

"I most solemnly swear that I will forever keep sacredly secret the signs, words and grips, and any and all other matters and knowledge of the Knights of the Ku Klux Klan regarding which a most rigid secrecy must be maintained, which may at any time be communicated to me, and will never divulge same nor even cause same to be divulged to any person in the whole world unless I know positively that such person is a member of this Order in good and regular standing and not even then unless it be for the best interest of this Order.

"I most sacredly vow and most positively swear that I will never yield to bribe, flattery, threats, passion, punishment, persecution, persuasion nor any enticements whatever coming from or offered by any person or persons, male or female, for the purpose of obtaining from me a secret or secret infor-

45

mation of the Knights of the Ku Klux Klan. I
will die rather than divulge same, so help me God.
Amen!"

(The candidate then waits till the Exalted Cyclops
and his Klan have decided to admit him. If this
is done, he is taken into the Klavern, and the oath
continues.)

Section III—*Fidelity*

"I, ——, before God and in the presence of these
mysterious Klansmen, on my sacred honor do most
solemnly and sincerely pledge, promise and swear
that I will diligently guard and faithfully foster
every interest of the Knights of the Ku Klux Klan
and will maintain its social caste and dignity.

"I swear I will never recommend any person for
membership in this Order whose mind is unsound or
whose reputation I know to be bad or whose character is doubtful or whose loyalty to our country is
in any way questionable.

"I swear that I will pay promptly all just and
legal demands made upon me to defray the expenses
of my Klan and this Order when same are due and
called for.

"I swear that I will protect the property of the
Knights of the Ku Klux Klan of any nature whatsoever and if any should be intrusted to my keeping

46

I will properly keep or rightly use same and will freely and promptly surrender same on official demand or if I am ever banished from or voluntarily discontinue my membership in this Order.

"I swear that I will most determinedly maintain peace and harmony in all the deliberations of the gatherings or assemblies of the Invisible Empire and of any subordinate jurisdiction or Klan thereof.

"I swear that I will most strenuously discourage selfishness and selfish political ambition on the part of myself or any Klansman.

"I swear that I will never allow personal friendship, blood or family relationship, nor personal, political or professional prejudice, malice nor ill will to influence me in casting my vote for the election or rejection of any applicant for membership in this Order, God being my helper.

AMEN!

SECTION IV—*Klannishness*

"I, ———, most solemnly pledge, promise and swear that I will never slander, defraud, deceive, or in any manner wrong the Knights of the Ku Klux Klan, a Klansman or a Klansman's family, nor will I suffer the same to be done if I can prevent it.

"I swear that I will be faithful in defending and protecting the home, reputation, and physical and business interest of a Klansman and that of Klansman's family.

"I swear that I will at any time, without hesitating, go to the assistance or rescue of a Klansman in any way at his call. I will answer. I will be truly Klannish toward Klansmen in all things honorable.

"I swear that I will never allow any animosity, friction nor ill will to arise and remain between myself and a Klansman, but will be constant in my efforts to promote real Klannishness among the members of this Order.

"I swear that I will keep secure to myself the secret of a Klansman when same is committed to me in the sacred bond of Klansmanship, the crime of violating THIS solemn oath, treason against the United States of America, rape and malicious murder alone excepted.

"I most solemnly assert and affirm that to the Government of the United States of America and any State thereof of which I may become a resident, I sacredly swear an unqualified allegiance above any other and every kind of government in the whole world. I here and now pledge my life, my property, my vote, and my sacred honor to uphold its flag, its constitution and constitutional laws and will protect, defend and enforce same unto death.

"I most Solemnly Promise and Swear That I will always, at all Times and in all places, Help, aid and assist, The duly Constituted officers of The law in The proper performance of Their Legal Duties.

"I swear that I will most zealously and valiantly shield and preserve by any and all justifiable means and methods the sacred constitutional rights and privileges of free public schools, free speech, free press, separation of church and state, liberty, white supremacy, just laws, and the pursuit of happiness against any encroachment of any nature by any person or persons, political party or parties, religious sect or people, native, naturalized or foreign, of any race, color, creed, lineage or tongue whatsoever.

"All of which I have sworn by THIS oath I will seal with my blood, be Thou my witness, Almighty God,

AMEN!"

I am informed, but have not been able to verify the statement, that in the fourth section on klannishness the two paragraphs which assert allegiance to the Government of the United States and which pledge aid to law officers, have been inserted recently. For those who are interested in puzzles let me point out the curious use of capitals in the section pledging support of law officers. It is very easy to suspect that these constitute some sort of a secret code, though I have heard no solution suggested.

The second important document of the Klan is its Constitution. Its most interesting sections are those which declare the purposes of the Order and limit its membership. These are as follows:

L'ENVOI

To the lovers of Law and Order, Peace and Justice, we send greeting; and to the shades of the valiant, venerated Dead, we gratefully and affectionately dedicate the

KNIGHTS OF THE KU KLUX KLAN

DECLARATION

"WE SOLEMNLY DECLARE TO ALL MANKIND that the Knights of the Ku Klux Klan, incorporated, is the original Ku Klux Klan organized in the year 1866, and active during the Reconstruction period of American history; and by and under its corporate name is revived, remodeled and expanded into a Ritualistic, Fraternal, Patriotic society of national scope, duly incorporated (under the laws of the State of Georgia) in the years 1915 and 1916, and dedicated to the same principles and spiritual purposes as more particularly set forth in Article II, of the Constitution and Laws of the Society.

50

OLD EVILS IN THE NEW KLAN

"WE DO FURTHER DECLARE TO THE WORLD that our original Prescript used as the governing law of the Ku Klux Klan, during the period of its former activities, and all official titles, mannerisms, usages and things therein prescribed have not been abandoned by us; but on the contrary, all of these, together with designs of paraphernalia, regalia, flags, banners, emblems, symbols, or other insignia and things prescribed or previously used by or under the authority of the Ku Klux Klan are the property of the Ku Klux Klan under and by virtue of its corporate name of Knights of the Ku Klux Klan and are held sacred by us as a precious heritage, which we shall jealously preserve, forever maintain and valiantly protect from profanation.

THE IMPERIAL PROCLAMATION

"To the lovers of Law, Order, Peace and Justice of all nations, People, Tribes and Tongues of the whole earth, Greetings:

"I, and the citizens of the Invisible Empire through me, make declaration to you:

"We, the members of this Order, desiring to promote patriotism toward our Civil Government; honorable peace among men and nations; protection for and happiness in the homes of our people; manhood, brotherhood, and love among ourselves, and liberty,

51

justice, and fraternity among all mankind; believing
we can best accomplish these noble purposes through
a mystic, social, patriotic, benevolent association,
having a perfected lodge system, with an exalted
ritualistic form of work and an effective form of
government, not for selfish profit, but for the mutual
betterment, benefit and protection of our oath-bound
associates, and their loved ones; do physically, socially,
morally and vocationally

PROCLAIM TO THE WORLD

"That we are dedicated to the sublime duty of providing generous aid, tender sympathy and fraternal
assistance amid fortune and misfortune in the efful-
gent light of life and amid the sable shadows of death;
and to the exalted privilege of demonstrating the practical utility of the great (yet most neglected) doctrine
of the Fatherhood of God and the Brotherhood of
man as a vital force in the lives and affairs of men.

"We invite all men who can qualify to become citizens of the Invisible Empire to approach the portal
of our beneficent domain, join us in our noble work
of extending its boundaries, and in disseminating the
gospel of 'Klankraft,' thereby encouraging, conserv-
ing, protecting and making vital the fraternal relationship in the practice of an honorable klannishness; to
share with us the glory of performing the sacred duty

of protecting womanhood; to maintain forever the God-given supremacy of the white race; to commemorate the holy and chivalric achievements of our fathers; to safeguard the sacred rights, privileges and institutions of our Civil Government; to bless mankind and to keep eternally ablaze the sacred fire of a fervent devotion to a pure Americanism.

"The Invisible Empire is founded on sterling character, and immutable principles based upon sacred sentiment and cemented by noble purposes. It is promoted by a sincere, unselfish devotion of the souls of men, and is governed by their consecrated intelligence. It is the soul of chivalry, virtue's impenetrable shield; and the devout impulse of an unconquered race.

"DONE IN THE AULIC OF HIS MAJESTY, the Emperor of the Invisible Empire, Knights of the Ku Klux Klan, in the Imperial Palace, in the Imperial City of Atlanta, Commonwealth of Georgia, United States of America.

This the 29th day of November, Anno Domini, Nineteen Hundred and Twenty-two Anno Klan LVI.

William Joseph Simmons

Emperor."

THE CHALLENGE OF THE KLAN

KU KLUX KREED

(Original Creed Revised)

"We, the Order of the Knights of the Ku Klux Klan, reverentially acknowledge the majesty and supremacy of Almighty God and recognize His goodness and providence through Jesus Christ our Lord.

"Recognizing our relation to the Government of the United States of America, the Supremacy of its Constitution, the Union of States thereunder, and the Constitutional Laws thereof, we shall ever be devoted to the sublime principles of a pure Americanism, and valiant in the defense of its ideals and institutions.

"We avow the distinction between the races of mankind as decreed by the Creator, and we shall ever be true to the maintenance of White Supremacy and strenuously oppose any compromise thereof.

"We appreciate the value of practical, fraternal relationship among men of kindred thought, purpose and ideals and the infinite benefits accruing therefrom; we shall faithfully devote ourselves to the practise of an honorable klannishness that the life of each may be a constant blessing to others.

OLD EVILS IN THE NEW KLAN

'NON SILBA SED ANTHAR'

PREAMBLE

"We, the members of this Order, citizens and probationers of the Invisible Empire, Knights of the Ku Klux Klan, in order to insure unity of organization; to guarantee an effective form of government; to perpetuate our great institution through patriotic and fraternal achievements; to preserve forever its holy principles; to continue and make vital its spiritual purposes; to achieve its laudable objects; to attain its lofty ideals; to consummate its mission and to promote effectively all things set forth in The Imperial Proclamation herein; do declare this Constitution of the Knights of the Ku Klux Klan, in lieu of the original Prescript of the Ku Klux Klan, as the supreme law of this Society, and pledge our voice, our loyalty, our manhood and our sacred honor to enforce the same. In our endeavor toward the faithful fulfillment of this, our honorable mission, we solemnly invoke the guidance and blessings of Almighty God in behalf of our country, our homes, our race and each other, now, and unto generations yet unborn.

55

APPELLATION AND GOVERNMENT

ARTICLE I

"*Section* 1. To the name of this Society, Ku Klux Klan, has been prefixed the words 'Knights of the,' and therefore forever hereafter it shall be known as 'KNIGHTS OF THE KU KLUX KLAN,' and is hereinafter referred to as, 'This Order.' It is, and shall continue to be, a Patriotic, Military, Benevolent, Ritualistic, Social and Fraternal Order or Society.

"*Section* 2. The government of this Order shall ever be military in character, especially in its executive management and control; and no legislative enactment or constitutional amendment hereafter shall encroach upon, affect or change this fundamental principle of the Invisible Empire.

"*Section* 3. The government of this Order shall be vested primarily in the Imperial Wizard, as Commander-in-Chief, who shall be supreme within the restrictions of this constitution, and as otherwise provided, and whose decisions, decrees, edicts, mandates, rulings and instructions shall be of full authority and unquestionably recognized and respected by each and every citizen of the Invisible Empire.

OLD EVILS IN THE NEW KLAN

OBJECTS AND PURPOSES

ARTICLE II

"Section 1. The objects of this Order shall be to unite white male persons, native-born Gentile citizens of the United States of America, who owe no allegiance of any nature or degree to any foreign government, nation, institution, sect, ruler, person or people; whose morals are good; whose reputations and vocations are respectable; whose habits are exemplary; who are of sound minds and eighteen years or more of age, under a common oath into a brotherhood of strict regulations; to cultivate and promote patriotism toward our Civil Government; to practise an honorable klannishness toward each other; to exemplify a practical benevolence; to shield the sanctity of the home and the chastity of womanhood; to maintain forever white supremacy, to teach and faithfully inculcate a high spiritual philosophy through an exalted ritualism, and by a practical devotion to conserve, protect and maintain the distinctive institutions, rights, privileges, principles, traditions and ideals of a pure Americanism.

"Section 2. To create and maintain an institution

by which the present and succeeding generations shall commemorate the great sacrifice, chivalric service and imperishable achievement of the 'Ku Klux Klan of the Reconstruction period of American History,' to the end that justice and honor be done the sacred memory of those who wrought through our mystic society during that period, and that their valiant accomplishments be not lost to posterity; to perpetuate their faithful courage, noble spirit, peerless principles and faultless ideals; to hold sacred and make effective their spiritual purpose in this and future generations; that they be rightly vindicated before the world by a revelation of the whole truth.

"*Section* 3. This Order is an institution of Chivalry, Humanity, Justice and Patriotism; embodying in its genius and principles all that is chivalric in conduct, noble in sentiment, generous in manhood, and patriotic in purpose. Its peculiar objects are: First, to protect the weak, the innocent, and the defenseless from the indignities, wrongs and outrages of the lawless, the violent and the brutal; to relieve the injured and the oppressed; to succor the suffering and unfortunate, especially widows and orphans. Second, to protect and defend the Constitution of the United States of America, and all laws passed in conformity thereto, and to protect the States and the people thereof from all invasion of their rights from any source whatsoever. Third, to aid and assist in the execution of all constitutional laws, and to preserve the honor and

58

dignity of the State by opposing tyranny, in any and every form or degree, from any and every source whatsoever, by a fearless and faithful administration of justice through due process of law; and to meet promptly and properly every behest of Duty without fear and without reproach.

TERRITORIAL JURISDICTIONS AND ASSEMBLIES

ARTICLE III

"*Section* 1. THE INVISIBLE EMPIRE: The phrase 'Invisible Empire' in a material sense denotes the universal geographical jurisdiction of this Order and it shall embrace the whole world. The convention of the Invisible Empire shall be known as the Imperial Klonvokation. The phrase 'Invisible Empire' in a spiritual sense applies to all the secrets and secret knowledge and information, secret work and working and things of this Order, and to all that has been, to all that now is and to all that is to be, the past, the present and the future, yesterday, to-day and forever; the dead of yesterday, the living of to-day, and the contemplated of to-morrow, of the life that now is and of that which is to come.

"*Section* 2. In a material sense, the territorial division of the Invisible Empire into a subordinate jurisdiction shall be known as a 'Realm,' and same shall embrace a State or States or a territorial possession of the United States of America, and shall derive its designation from that State or Territory which it embraces, and its number shall be given it in order of its formation. The convention of a Realm shall be known as the 'Klorero.'

"*Section* 3. A territorial division of a Realm shall be known as a 'Province,' and shall embrace a county or a number of counties of a State. Provinces shall be designated by number. The convention of a Province shall be known as a 'Klonverse.'

"*Section* 4. A 'Klan' is the unit of this Order; it is the local or subordinate body, lodge, or organization, and its territorial jurisdiction shall be known as the 'Klanton' which shall extend in all directions to a distance midway between the location of the Klan and the nearest Klan thereto, except as otherwise designated by the Imperial Wizard or Grand Dragon of a Realm. The boundaries of a Klanton shall be fixed, so far as is possible, on the delivery of the Klan charter. A convention or an assembly of a Klan in secret session shall be known as the 'Klonklave.'

"*Section* 5. All things and matters which do not exist within this Order or are not authorized by or do not come under its jurisdiction shall be designated as the 'Alien World.' All persons who are not members of this Order shall be designated as 'Aliens.'

MEMBERSHIP

ARTICLE IV

"*Section* 1. The qualifications for membership in this Order shall be: An applicant must be a white male Gentile person, a native-born citizen of the United States of America who owes no allegiance of any nature or degree whatsoever to any foreign government, nation, institution, sect, ruler, prince, potentate, people or person; he must have attained the age of eighteen years, be of sound mind, good character, of commendable reputation and respectable vocation, a believer in the tenets of the Christian Religion, and one whose allegiance, loyalty and devotion to the Government of the United States of America in all things is unquestionable. He must be a resident within the jurisdiction of the Klan to which he applies, for at least twelve months immediately preceding the date of his application for citizenship, provided, however, that special dispensation may be granted by the Grand Dragon of that Realm in organized Realms, or by the Imperial Wizard in unorganized Realms, to waive this condition.

"*Section* 2. Applications for membership in this Order must be on a regular charter petition by charter applicants of a Klan, and on a regular application blank after a Klan has been chartered. The applicant must state whether he ever has applied for membership in this Order, and such application made to a chartered Klan must be endorsed by at least two Klansmen, or by a Kleagle or by the Imperial Wizard of this Order.

"*Section* 3. The 'Klectokon' (initiation fee) is given by an applicant and accepted by this Order as a donation to its propagation and general fund and not in the sense of purchasing membership in this Order by the applicant, and this donation must accompany each application for citizenship. The Klectokon is a sum of money of not less than Ten ($10.00) Dollars, nor more than Twenty-five ($25.00) Dollars.

"*Section* 4. All men who served as members of the Original Ku Klux Klan or rendered direct service thereto, or who were so connected with similar organizations during the Reconstruction period of American history shall be admitted to full fellowship in this Order without payment of Klectokon or dues; provided, however, they individually qualify for membership under the requirements of Section 1 of this Article.

"*Section* 5. An applicant's qualifications must be known before he is accepted for membership in this Order. Great care must be exercised on the part of a Kleagle or a Klan in ascertaining an applicant's qualifications under Section 1, of this Article."

OLD EVILS IN THE NEW KLAN

The rest of the Constitution is devoted to details of the organization, the duties of officers, etc.* It shows what seems a complete inconsistency in the Klan, since the form of its government is that of an absolute despotism, although the Klan puts itself forward as the one champion of democracy. The Imperial Wizard has enormous power and can veto the election of any officer, or remove him at will, except that he must grant a trial to Imperial officials—his "Genii." His term of office is fixed at four years, but his election is by the Grand Dragons, and these he appoints himself and can remove instantly. Thus it seems impossible ever to remove him, however dangerous he may become.

His power over all members, if they keep their oaths, is considerable. They promise to "heed" all his commands; I find in the Constitution no limit on these commands, though there may be some in the Kloran—the ritual. But there is no doubt that he has a very complete, uncontrolled constitutional power, and that he can produce sudden, secret and concentrated action when he wishes. How far he could go is another matter; there are many things he could not do without violating his oath and thus releasing his followers.

One more Klan document which is not official is worth reading. It is called "A Klansman's Creed" and is published frequently in Klan newspapers. It

* It will be found in the Appendix.

63

seems to state very fairly the beliefs of a large proportion of the membership.

A KLANSMAN'S CREED

I believe in God and the tenets of the Christian religion and that a godless nation can not long prosper.

I believe that a church that is not grounded on the principles of morality and justice is a mockery to God and to man.

I believe that a church that does not have the welfare of the common people at heart is unworthy.

I believe in the eternal separation of Church and State.

I hold no allegiance to any foreign government, emperor, king, pope or any other foreign, political or religious power.

I hold my allegiance to the Stars and Stripes next to my allegiance to God alone.

I believe in just laws and liberty.

I believe in the upholding of the Constitution of these United States.

I believe that our Free Public School is the cornerstone of good government and that those who are seeking to destroy it are enemies of our Republic and are unworthy of citizenship.

I believe in freedom of speech.

I believe in a free press uncontrolled by political parties or by religious sects.

I believe in law and order.

I believe in the protection of our pure womanhood.

I do not believe in mob violence, but I do believe that laws should be enacted to prevent the causes of mob violence.

I believe in a closer relationship of capital and labor.

I believe in the prevention of unwarranted strikes by foreign labor agitators.

I believe in the limitation of foreign immigration.

I am a native-born American citizen and I believe my rights in this country are superior to those of foreigners.

One further ground for criticism is inherent in the Klan; the possibility that the members may feel oathbound to protect other Klansmen from justice. The

65

oath reads: "I swear that I will keep secure to my-self a secret of a Klansman when same is committed to me in the sacred bond of Klansmanship, the crime of violating this sacred oath, treason against the United States of America, rape and malicious murder alone excepted." This seems fairly flat and not likely to assist any one who might attempt to bring Klans-men to justice for ordinary crimes.

There is also to be considered the most serious criticism that can be made against the Klan: that it is based wholly on class division, race and religious prejudice and hatred in general. The validity of this criticism depends so much on the actual propaganda, and is so involved with its purpose and programme, that it must be left for a later chapter.

Of course there is a Klan defense for all this. In the first place many of these same charges can be, and have been, brought against other secret orders. There was a time, now almost forgotten, when the Masonic Order was under just this kind of attack. I have seen old books which accused it of almost every crime in the calendar, including treason and "ritual murder." Within a few years a book was printed in London alleging that Masonry was responsible for the Terror in the French Revolution and at least partly responsible for Bolshevism. So, to a large extent, the Klan in these matters is on all fours with other secret orders.

Then, too, the section of the oath quoted above is

66

in conflict with other sections. The Klansman also swears unqualified allegiance to the United States Government, support of the laws, and aid to law officers. So he has at least a choice under his oath whether he will protect another Klansman from the law. Dr. Evans believes there is no conflict—that the enforcement of the law is unquestionably first. But there is some talk in the Klan of changing the phraseology.

I put to Dr. Evans, as bluntly as I could, all these objections to the Klan. He discussed them very frankly and admitted some grounds for most of them, as well as explaining and justifying them. Though he did not say so, I gathered that he feels some of them are a heavy incubus left over from the evil days of the Simmons-Clark régime. But when I asked whether he did not think it a mistake to have revived the old Klan, with all the old associations, he said he did not.

"It was necessary in launching the movement to have some form of appeal which would give an immediate grip on the imagination of men," he declared. "The South's love of the old Klan did it. We have now reached the point where the ancient history is less important, and where the name 'Knight of the Ku Klux Klan' is held sacred by every Klansman and is the medium through which he expects to express his Americanism."

"Does not the obligation of the Klan oath to protect

the Klansman in any secret except one involving treason, malicious murder, or rape, actually prevent the
punishment of any Klansman guilty of crime, when
the evidence necessary to his conviction is in the hands
of other Klansmen?" I asked.

"There is nothing in the obligation of the Klansman
that requires him under the oath to protect another
Klansman in any secret that would conflict with his
duty to his government or with his oath of allegiance
to the constituted officers of the law. There has been
much discussion on this point, and in order to have
the matter perfectly clear, the particular part of the
oath referred to, officially quoted, is as follows:

" 'I SWEAR THAT I WILL KEEP SECURE TO MY-
SELF A SECRET OF A KLANSMAN WHEN SAME IS
COMMITTED TO ME IN THE SACRED BOND OF KLANS-
MANSHIP, THE CRIME OF VIOLATING THIS SOLEMN
OATH—TREASON AGAINST THE UNITED STATES OF
AMERICA—RAPE AND MALICIOUS MURDER ALONE
EXCEPTED.'

"This, upon reading, will reveal that the Klansman
merely pledges himself to hold secure to himself information pertaining to a Klansman from the outside
world, and in no way refers to protection of a Klansman or the maintenance of the secret of a Klansman when he has violated the law." Dr. Evans then
quoted to me also the sections in relation to alleged
allegiance and law enforcement which appear in the
text of the oath already given.

OLD EVILS IN THE NEW KLAN

I asked his justification for secrecy. He had admitted that it might involve some serious evils.

"In the present state of the country, when it is necessary to combat organizations using these and even worse methods," he said, "it would be foolish to surrender an advantage.

"Then, too, in the early days of an organization which is putting forward any strong programme or doctrine which is new and controversial, there is danger of retaliation against individual members. When it becomes stronger this danger becomes less.

"The Klan will be out in the open one of these days. It is practically so now in some places. It will unmask, and it will make public its membership at any time that those forces which are throttling American ideals and diluting our American citizenship and living under their own interpretation—if they have any!—of the Constitution, come into the spotlight of American publicity and reveal their intentions and motives and when legislation is made all-inclusive. This applies to political as well as to religious organizations."

"Does not secrecy encourage lawlessness in Klansmen?" I persisted.

"That argument is fallen to the ground," he said. "Statistics show most marvelous improvement in crime conditions. In Louisiana they have thirty per cent. less crime since the Klan became strong there. In Texas there is less law violation then ever before, and there are more convictions. Lynching has become a thing of the past."

"Does not secrecy at least give opportunity and protection for lawlessness?" was my next question.

"Men with unlawful purposes may have thought so and have tried to get somewhere where they could violate the law without punishment. The idea of secrecy itself operates negatively within the Klan, so far as this question is concerned. In fact such action is contrary to the Klansman's oath, and the spirit of the Klan is such that a Klansman wishing to commit violence would be more likely to conceal it from his fellow-members than to ask their assistance. The laws of the Order are drawn to prevent any private or unauthorized use of the hood and the gown.

"I will add that if any such danger does exist the cure is not in attacking the Klan, but in providing heavy punishment for violation of the law. The law should not attempt to legislate against harmless uses of the mask, but should provide heavy penalties for conspiracy to violate the law and make a special crime to cover lawlessness when in disguise."

"Does not the Klansman's oath of secrecy which prevents his admitting his membership in the Order when called for jury service, operate against the proper administration of justice?"

"No," he declared. "A Klansman will answer the call of justice in any court at any time. No Klansman to our knowledge has ever been asked, when being questioned for jury service, whether he was or was not a Klansman but has answered in the affirmative. Naturally the question arises and brings up the point that if it is the practise of legal procedure that jurymen be asked this question, then the right to ask concerning all fraternal and religious affiliations, would be at least consistent. Very few judges consider this question as relevant."

"Does not the obligation of the Klansman, and also the general respect or fear in which the Klan is held by public officials, tend to the acquittal of Klansmen brought to the bar?" I asked. There is considerable evidence, which will be presented in a later chapter, that this is the case, although that evidence does not imply that this is deliberately caused by Klan officials. Dr. Evans, however, denies it, and probably hopes that his denial is true.

"No, if it did it would be a severe indictment of the public officials themselves," he said. "There is no more need for a public official in the exercise of his duties to fear a Klansman than there is for him to fear a Republican or a Democrat; not as much, because both political parties are in politics and the Klan is not.

"It is true that anonymous communications are often used by individuals in an attempt to intimidate public officials and sometimes private persons, but not a single case is on record where they have been traced back to the Klan or proved to be from an original authoritative Klan source. The Klan will certainly uphold any official in the carrying out of the responsibilities of his office, probably more so were he under anonymous threats than were he not."

But when I asked what value there is for the Klan in "bedsheets and pillow cases"; if they are not to create terror, the doctor first laughed, and then grew grave.

"They are very valuable as an advertising feature," he said. "But though they may seem to the public mind to be merely 'bedsheets and pillow cases,' they certainly do not so seem to the Klansman. They are regalia, they carry to him important significance and typify certain ideals that are as old as the ages themselves. They are just as sacred to him as the fez and the plume are to the Masons, as other religious regalia are to the church, and as uniforms and flags are in governmental functions. They occupy the same place as a means of impressiveness in the conferring of degrees that other fraternal regalia do in other organizations.

"It is true that they have a certain psychological appeal and have undoubtedly proved their value in the propagation of the Knights of the Ku Klux Klan. This appeal as an advertising feature is changed into something far different in the mind of any individual as soon as he has joined the Klan, has become informed, and appreciates their significance as regalia.

OLD EVILS IN THE NEW KLAN

He grew grave again when I asked what the Klan means by "Invisible Empire."

"We are dropping the expression," he replied, "using it less and less. It is a ritualistic phrase referring to the geographical jurisdiction of the Order. It has no reference to any political government."

"Is not the government of the Klan a complete dictatorship?" I asked.

"In form, yes. In actuality, no," he declared. "It is necessary to have that form of government, as a democracy, unless organized, can not protect nor cleanse itself. Also, the only way to protect the Klan from constant efforts to exploit it for personal profit, or from demagogues who might be able to sway a portion of its membership through an appeal to emotion, is to have a government strong enough to suppress all such attempts.

"But actually, in spite of the form of constitution, it would be impossible for an Imperial officer to run counter to the wishes of the organization as a whole. While the body of the organization is secret, the officers and their conduct are out in the open, subject to constant watchfulness. If they go wrong they will lose their following, and the organization be destroyed. There have been instances in which this has been proved.

"I will add that this form of organization is common to all fraternities, and that the Klan is no more centralized than even some religious bodies which are never attacked on that ground. Still, there is an apparent contradiction here. The Klan stands for democracy in government, and must also stand for democracy inside itself. A solution is being sought."

"Is not some of the language in the oaths and constitution such that it suggests violence, at least to certain types of mind?" I asked.

"I do not believe so. Few people understand the spiritual vision of a Klansman. Any individual who had that idea in mind would, I believe, be promptly disabused of it in the obligations and interpretations of the very first ceremony."

"Does not the secrecy of the Klan show cowardice?" was the last of my hectoring questions to the Imperial Wizard.

"I think your question is unfair," was his reply. "But I will answer it. At Carnegie, Pennsylvania, unarmed Klansmen took the bullets of the un-American alien forces unflinchingly and did not precipitate a riot. At Perth Amboy, New Jersey, Klansmen when cornered in a small room by a mob of from five to eight thousand aliens, stacked their arms in the center of the room, walked out into the crowd under reported police assistance, where they stood a steady barrage of brickbats, bullets and other missiles, many being unmercifully beaten. But they did not resist, knowing that such resistance would cause bloodshed. Innumerable cases of this kind are evidence of what we believe to be the greatest moral courage."

OLD EVILS IN THE NEW KLAN

In his discussion of the ritual of the Klan, the grotesque nomenclature and the symbolism of the Order, I confess that Dr. Evans got beyond my depth. I have never been a member of any secret order, and what I have been able to see of their ceremonies has never seemed very sacred to me. Yet I am forced to consider this a blindness in myself, for I have friends, sane and intelligent, to whom these things are very solemn and very sacred. Certainly they are both of these things to Dr. Evans, and his reverent attitude made me ashamed of having referred to the "Klan menagerie." I can only give his reply to my question as he made it.

"I probably can not explain in a way that would be fully understood by any one outside fraternal societies," he said. "The best answer I can give is this: that, just as the spiritual ideals of religion have to be clothed in formalities which to the non-religious man seem ludicrous and are ridiculed, so it is necessary to clothe the idealism and spiritual concepts of fraternalism, and especially of a purposeful Order such as the Klan, in similar ritualism and formalism.

"I will leave it to some psychologist to explain why that is so, but every man with experience in dealing with ideals on a popular basis knows that the people want and need symbolism and that when it is destroyed, something precious, vital and irreplaceable has been taken away from them. For myself, I know that if there is a question about the literal inspiration

75

of any word in the Bible I do not want to consider it.
I wish to believe. I do believe. It is only on this
basis that one can understand the formalism of the
Klan."

His idea, by the way, received support from a very
different quarter only two days after this talk. Dr.
W. M. Guthrie, Rector of St. Mark's-on-the-Bouwerie,
New York, demanded from his pulpit an increase in
ritualism in religion, declaring that without it "all
we have are sickly doctrines."

To return to Dr. Evans—my last question to him
along this line was whether the Klan would not become extremely dangerous if ever perverted.

"It would," he declared. "It would be frightful.
But the very organization of the Klan is such that
if the attempt were ever made, it would automatically
destroy itself. The strength of the Klan is in the
ideals of the Klansmen, and that strength can not be
used apart from those ideals."

Some matters Dr. Evans did not wish to discuss
for publication. "Let's leave that for a while—I'm
not ready for that yet," he would say. Finally he
made a blanket statement, indicating that his reforms
are not ended, and that he plans changes in the Constitution which will remove some of the grounds for
criticism, perhaps most.

"There are certain difficulties inherent in the growth
of the organization and its form and the language
of some of its official documents," he said. "These

naturally must be handled slowly and with great care. They are being handled in this fashion and will be corrected. But I do not care to discuss them for publication until solutions have been reached."

Whatever these reforms may be, they naturally can not be taken into consideration until they are made effective. Judgment for the time being must be based on the Klan as it is. And, from the facts available, it seems clear that the Klan to-day is still irresponsible, uncontrollable, autocratic, and terroristic in form; that if its members keep their oaths and take them and some of the official language and formulas literally, and are impressed by the apparent meaning of its symbolism, it is quite capable of becoming a real invisible government, protecting its members from the law and striking powerfully and with immunity from the dark. It seems that General Forrest and his associates in 1868 had good reason to destroy such an organization the moment their desperate emergency passed. It can be justified to-day only by the belief that there is a new emergency demanding drastic methods.

The great present safeguard—the reason why all these evils are apparent and only partly actual—is in the leadership and control. The danger will remain until the organization itself is changed. From meeting and seeing many Klansmen I know that a very large proportion have joined in spite of these features of the Klan, not because of them. That they have joined at all is proof of the power of appeal of the present purposes and programme. Dr. Evans is right when he says that the strength of the Klan to-day is in the ideals of the Klansmen.

CHAPTER IV

THE CRUSADE OF THE FIERY CROSS

THE Ku Klux Klan, like all the rest of us, is quite naturally at its best when seen through its ambitions, purposes and ideals. In them it can ignore and escape from all bad habits, evil traditions, discrepancies in practise and failures in conduct, and appear in its Sunday best. Of course, this is a great deal better than its working clothes, but the Klan shares a very common failing if it wishes to be judged entirely by it. Certainly, in reaching a verdict on any human thing, purpose as well as practise must be considered.

These ideals and aspirations are beyond question the Klan's strongest point. It is they that have brought in so many hundreds of thousands of members in the last few months and are now bringing in 100,000 every week. The record proves that they, and not the ritual, the allure of night-riding, nor the pleasure of hating other races or sects, are the real appeal of the Klan. All these were offered by the

Klan under the Simmons-Clark régime, yet after seven years it claimed only 90,000 members. Evans, who has given form and spirit to the new ideas, has rallied millions in a single year!

Many things that he says sound like platitudes, to be sure. They are, nevertheless, highly important. They are the ideals and aspirations of the "most average man in America," and America is the country of the average man. In it there is no idea more powerful than a well-chosen and well-aimed platitude.

Dr. Evans explained his ideals carefully to me in the first interview he has ever given for publication on this subject. He broke his long standing rule of silence because he is now confident of his organization; satisfied that it has been made over so that it is safe from effective criticism, and is ready for great things. He is ready, too, therefore, to tell about it. He spoke partly, also, because of urgings for publicity from the great northern wing of the Klan, men to whom the old traditions mean less than nothing, and who are smarting under criticism they believe to be ignorant and unfair.

I talked with Dr. Evans for several hours in his "aulic" in the Imperial Palace in Atlanta, and later for more hours in Washington. He talked freely and apparently frankly, and the statements which follow were carefully worded to express the thought brought out in the two long discussions. The actual wording is sometimes that of his advisers, for he himself has a tendency to oratorical prolixity, but the thought is always his.

I have often been asked whether Dr. Evans is sincere in his ideals and purposes. That is beyond my power to determine, but I personally believe that he is. He often reminds me of a rough-and-ready evangelist. He has most of the tricks, including the—"Brother, I'll say to you—" with which he began many of his statements. But whether sincere or not, it is certain that he believes fully in the power of these ideas, not only to win support and recruits, but to hold men and achieve results.

"I'll tell you, Brother," he said again and again, "you don't realize the power of the Klan ideal. It makes men over. The Klan idea is the most potent thought in America to-day."

"Suppose you define that idea exactly," I finally demanded. "What, in your mind, is the Klan to-day —its central idea and general purpose? What are the 'ideals of the Klansmen' which you say are its real strength?"

"The Klan is an organization to promote practical patriotism—Americanism," he replied without hesitation. "Its ideal is to restore and then to preserve and develop the old, fundamental ideas on which the nation was founded and which have made it great; to provide for the uncontaminated growth of Anglo-Saxon civilization. This, historically and instinctively, involves racial purity, free Christian thought

81

(which is possible only under Protestanism), liberty under law with full regard for the rights of others, a complete and unselfish acceptance of the duties and burdens of citizenship as well as its privileges, and a spirit of democracy which considers the good of the nation as a whole instead of merely the interest of any class, race, religion, group, bloc, or any other special and limited body."

This, naturally, did not fit at all with my previous notions of the Klan.

"Your critics," I pointed out, "will say that actually you are merely setting up another bloc; that the only way by which the group that exists can be broken up is through education."

"Every one knows that education, so far, has failed to do this," he answered. "The Klan, in fact, is trying to educate the hostile elements in two ways; first, by showing the value and the beauty of true citizenship, and second by insisting that every new citizen shall have had the benefit of an American education, and shall thus have learned Americanism from his youth up. In the meanwhile—till this education is effective—the Klan is merely recognizing facts as they exist. If it is setting up a new group, it is at least a group which in time can absorb every real citizen, and it is the only group which even pretends to do this. And, until education does its work, the Klan is the only body in a position to protect fundamental Americanism."

THE CRUSADE OF THE FIERY CROSS

"Well, then, considering the Klan as a reform—a crusade—what are the conditions in American political and social life which demand such a crusade today?" I asked.

"First and foremost, it is because Americans have neglected their public duty," he replied. "Three out of ten of our native-born citizens—and until I became a Klansman I was one of them—have taken the advantages of American liberties and free government for granted. They did not either give them the thought nor take the trouble regarding them that are essential if they are to be maintained. Heretofore, the average citizen has been born into conditions and environments which were accepted without thought or regard to the fundamental principles involved. Not so with a Klansman. He does not accept a given condition of affairs, regardless of how long standing or how great the authority therefor, but searches out truth and facts. The need of the Klan is the same as the need of America for this kind of thought.

"In the second place, there is the immediate and alarming fact that American thought and life have been and are being perverted from their true course by excessive alien mixtures. It is foolish to expect, and it has been proved wrong by experience to hope, that people of alien races, with different traditions, different education and different ideals which are bred into them both by inheritance and training, can within a few years understand America, the American spirit or the American ideals. America stands for a definite form of government and of social organization and of thought, which have been developed through centuries and which are, therefore, an essential part of and are fitted to the American people. It is no reflection on other peoples that they are different, but it is a fact that they are and that the attempts which they make to subvert American thought to their own traditions are threatening the most fundamental factors in American life.

"We believe that only those who have been born or educated in America to American ideals of society and home can intelligently conceive and apply Americanism in its true sense."

"What specific reform does the Klan hope to make?" was my next question. "In other words, what are its direct objectives?"

Dr. Evans' answer to this question may be taken as the official platform of the Klan.

"The Klan hopes to inculcate the fundamental principles of the Klan doctrine and the application thereof into the minds of the American people to the extent that all groups will become assimilated into a solidified American electorate expressing the will of the American people, who will then form their own curative remedies for specific evils," he began.

I interrupted to point out that this was rather vague, but he swept me aside and went on.

"Specifically, the Klan plans the education of the

great mass of its own members and at the same time of all American citizens, to the responsibilities as well as privileges of citizenship; the development of an operative patriotism, which is nothing more nor less than the full understanding and expression of the duties of citizens. Heretofore, this education has been primarily within the organization, and has been reflected only in a small measure to the outside world. No greater duty nor greater responsibility could be accepted by any group than the furtherance of these principles and the development of an educational programme of enlightenment to all America.

"Secondly, the Klan aims to protect the American electorate from further dilution by alien elements which by racial and religious barriers resist assimilation, by restricting the franchise to men and women who are able, through birth and education, to understand Americanism. This means practically a restriction to native-born children who have had the benefit of the training given by the American educational system and who are thus by birth and education fundamentally equipped for the responsibilities of citizenship and the right of franchise.

"Third, the Klan aims to protect the nation from any further evils of unassimilated and unassimilable elements through an immediate and complete stopping of immigration, the stoppage to remain complete until reason appears again for accepting foreign immigration.

THE CHALLENGE OF THE KLAN

"As to the National Government: There has been a wide-spread feeling among Klansmen that in the last few years the operation of the National Government has shown weaknesses indicating a possible need of rather fundamental reform. This is shown by the fact that in election after election the decision has been based on dissatisfaction with and protest against previous workings of the Government, rather than on any constructive thought or a referendum upon specific pledges for constructive and corrective governmental measures. The immediate programme of the Klan is to point out certain fundamental conditions in the Governmennt and bring before the American electorate definite constructive facts upon which the voters may predicate an intelligent expression of the will of the American people.

"Locally, the Klan stands for law enforcement, the election of competent and conscientious officials, state and city, the elimination of private graft and spoils hunting of all kinds, and the immediate and vigorous improvement of the public schools by securing necessary funds and in every other way working to advance and perpetuate the public schools of our states and counties."

Leaving Dr. Evans for a moment, the perspective from which this programme of the Klan is viewed may be cleared a little by going back to compare it with the ideas around which the Know-nothing movement was formed. That movement took for its motto

86

THE CRUSADE OF THE FIERY CROSS

—"Americans must rule," and for its countersign the supposed command of Washington—"Place none but Americans on guard to-night." Another slogan often used was—"Shall foreign influence rule? NEVER!" And in its platform of 1855 when it came into the open as a political party, there were provisions for the following:

Acknowledgment of an Almighty Being.
Development of an intense American feeling.
Maintenance of the Union and opposition to sectionalism (this was an attempt to straddle on the slavery question).
Obedience to the Constitution and laws.
Restrictions on Immigration.
Opposition to political corruption.
Resistance to Roman Catholic church and
Teaching of the Bible in the Public Schools.

When Dr. Evans outlined his platform, my mind went back to the second and third points in the Know-nothing platform.

"Can not a Jew, Roman Catholic or Negro be a good citizen," I asked.

"According to their capabilities they could," he answered. "The Klan has no bitterness toward any one of these people. The Klan is simply standing for certain principles and it thinks that these principles can best be exemplified by people possessing certain qualifications and beliefs. There is no reflection on others who may be very patriotic, but the Klan thinks that for obvious reasons people born and educated under true American ideals think more of this country and typify a higher degree of patriotism than others. The Klan has no monopoly on patriotism any more than any other person or organization has a monopoly on any other good thing, but it is selecting as members, men with certain good qualifications and this is done every day by other organizations without objection or comment.

"This right of selection is made to seem to draw the inference that Catholics, Jews and Negroes are not equally good citizens. This is not true. The Klan will condemn no man or set of men so long as he or they are obedient to law and uphold the principles of Americanism and the principles of the Christian religion."

"What is the basis," I pursued, "for the discrimination which the Klan makes against members of these races and religions?"

"Simply this," Dr. Evans replied. "One places a limitation on his citizenship by a religious principle which precludes possibility of separation of church and state. The other, for two thousand years, has rigidly adhered to a racial limitation and to an avoidance of intermarriage which makes it impossible for him to be assimilated into American life wholly and unreservedly.

"As to the Negro, America must face the fact that

THE CRUSADE OF THE FIERY CROSS

God Almighty never intended social equality for Negro and white man. The Negro is America's problem and we should give him all the privileges we can give, but face squarely the issue that intermarriage and social equality are impossible. Now that the passions and prejudices of the Civil War are so long past, this can be done. The Negro is separated from the white man by a profound racial barrier and many centuries of civilization. The racial difference completely bars any thought of social equality, because that would be impossible without intermingling; the lack of mental development can not possibly be overcome by any immediate process of education. America owes it to the Negro to give him every privilege and protection, and every opportunity consistent with our national safety. But we dare not risk the destruction of our civilization, which might come about if its control should ever fall into the Negro's hands.

"I would say that individual members of any of the classes referred to might be patriotic citizens, and that there have been instances in which they have shown very high patriotism. But America to-day is threatened very definitely; there is need for immediate organization to meet the danger, and the surest way of making certain that our organization will be free from alien influences is to issue the same order that Washington did: 'Put none but Americans on guard to-night!'"

"How will the Klan try to put its programme into

effect?" was the next question. "What are its strategy and tactics?"

"The Klan attempts to educate and influence its members to vote for the best candidate regardless of party, in every political contest," was his reply. "And it provides them with full and specific information about all candidates and issues to enable them to form individual opinions. It does not indorse any party or any candidates nor any issues except those I have specifically outlined. It is clear that the Klan programme must result in political action, and that it can be carried out in no other way. But this action is sought purely through education and not through direct attempt to control votes.

"The Klan objective is to inculcate the fundamental principles of Klan doctrine, but the application thereof must come from the people themselves.

"In actual operation it would appear that the Klan functions along the same lines as the Anti-Saloon League. This means that it does not affiliate with any party but that by persistently supporting men of certain types and beliefs, opposing men of un-American types and beliefs and working for the defeat of officials who have failed in public duty or in Americanism, it strives to make certain, and to make politicians understand that America is to be ruled locally and nationally by Americans, decently and solely in the interests of America.

"Undoubtedly, as in other large organizations, there

have been and will be attempts to pervert the power of the Klan to selfish ends, to personal ambitions. Those which have already occurred have been dealt with by the removal of the guilty men from office in the Klan, and future cases will be handled with the utmost severity."

"How active is the Klan in politics now, both directly and indirectly?" I asked.

"The Klan is and always will be active politically," he said. "The form of its organization and the nature of its objective automatically insure that its chief expression will be found in the political field. It is not, however, in politics in the usual sense of the word; that is, it has no political ambitions or desires for itself or its officials."

Dr. Evans said much more, but this, I believe, gives a fair and reasonably complete outline of Klan purposes and programme as he sees them and as he wants the country to see them. But, to complete the understanding, there should be taken into consideration also the definitions given in shorter and somewhat uglier words by two other leading Klansmen. It must be remembered that they have no official right to speak for the Klan, but they do speak for thousands.

"The real idea of the Klan," said the first of them, a lawyer and reform politician, "is to make this a white man's country once more, and then keep it that way. A 'white man' means people of our own breed! Other parts of the programme are important just so far as they contribute to that. But to do this it means that we must have good officials, because a man who will cater to any kind of corruption will be in reach of anti-American influences. The best way to do this is to get native white Americans into office. I don't pretend that's a sure cure, but it will raise the average. If that is done, then we have to contend only with natural stupidity and natural crookedness, but not with definitely hostile influences which become more dangerous the more intelligent the official is. The next part of the job will be to pick the best men among the Americans."

The other definition is even shorter. It was made by a New York physician—an official of a Fifth Avenue Church.

"Everybody knows that politicians nowadays cater to all kinds of 'elements,' mostly selfish, some corrupt and some definitely anti-American," he declared. "They cater to the German vote, the Catholic vote, the Jewish vote, the Italian vote, the bootleg vote, the vice vote, and sometimes even to the violently criminal vote. What the Klan intends to do is to make them pay some attention to the American vote, the Protestant Christian vote and the decent, God-fearing, law-abiding vote!"

I have found no one ready to deny that in the Klan programme, as thus laid down, there is much that is sound and a great deal that is fine and patriotic.

There must be, since it is winning so many decent citizens.

Criticism of it rests on two grounds, both of which have a very large basis in fact.

The first is that this programme is not sincere, and that the Klan in operation is very different from the Klan in protestation. That question will be taken up in the chapters telling of the actual working of the organization.

The other is that, even if the ideas set forth are sincere, and even if the Klan did fully live up to them, they are extremely dangerous, because through and under them there run certain basic concepts as old as history, almost instincts, which have come to the surface often and have always proved so terrible and destructive that only the greatest need can justify bringing them to life again. These are the ideas of class, race and religious division, with all their lurking devils of discord, prejudice, hatred and strife. These ideas, the situation they create, and the Klan's defense for its use of them will be taken up in the next chapter.

CHAPTER V

INVOKING THE WHIRLWIND

THERE are certain states of mind, shared by most men, which are so dangerous and devastating whenever they take possession of large groups that the most daring of leaders hesitates to invoke them. History always links them with storms of prejudice, discord, hatred and strife. They are almost impossible to compromise and they can hardly be discussed without rancor, so by common consent as civilization has advanced they have been more and more pushed into the background of thought for the sake of peace and quiet.

The most dangerous of these spring from the ideas of exclusive and militant race, or national, or religious unity. Each carries with it a record of bloodshed, terror, persecution and unspeakable horror that staggers the mind.

Yet the Ku Klux Klan has gathered all three into one bundle, and is invoking the whirlwind they always bring—and hoping to control it—as the basis for its attempt to reform America!

94

This is, in fact, the really distinctive thing about the Klan. One may work for law enforcement, better education, better government or any of the other reforms at which the Klan aims, through a myriad of other organizations. But in no other will one find the programme and the very form of the organization itself based on the exclusive Americanism of "native, white, Protestant" supremacy.

The Klan makes its position on this perfectly clear. It is one place where there is complete harmony between its formulæ and its thought and practise. These ideas run through all its documents, acts and speech; they are present, sometimes spoken and sometimes implied, in every discussion of the Klan by its leaders. They are the very soul of the movement.

A few quotations from the official documents already cited show this:

"To maintain forever the God given supremacy of the white race . . . the devout impulse of an unconquered race."—*Proclamation of the Klan Constitution.*

"We avow the distinction between the races of man as decreed by the Creator, and we shall ever be true to the maintenance of White Supremacy and strenuously oppose any compromise thereof."— *Ku Klux Kreed.*

"The objects of this Order shall be to unite all white male persons, native-born Gentile citizens of the United States of America, who owe no allegiance of any nature or degree to any foreign gov-

95

ernment, nation, institution, sect, ruler, person or people . . . to maintain forever white supremacy . . . to conserve, protect and maintain the distinctive institutions, rights, privileges, principles, traditions and ideals of a pure Americanism."—*Klan Constitution—Art. II—Section* I. (Most of this is repeated in the provisions regarding membership.)

Thus the Klan calls the devils from the vasty deep. And they have come. It is safe to say that to every man in the Klan these ideas *in some form* are a compelling motive. With many they are so refined as to take the shape of reasoned convictions; with most they are instinctive—with some, savage. The reforms made by Dr. Evans have aimed to keep them under control, to handle them without hatred, to restrict the damage they may do, but they have not removed them. The Klan stands and must stand till it dies, for "native, white, Protestant supremacy."

In most discussion of the Klan all argument ends at this point, if it ever gets past the old talk of graft and night-riding. To Jews, Roman Catholics, Negroes and aliens, and to all the vast numbers whose sympathies are still with the alien elements in our population, there can hardly be further debate. The movement is, on its face, hostile to them.

For many others, especially of the sentimental liberal variety, this is also enough. They had fondly believed that such ideas were practically dead, and they hate the Klan merely because it has upset their

minds. But to a far higher type of mind the fact
that the Klan is using dangerous ideas and is making
trouble, carries sufficient condemnation.

But this is not quite enough. Sound judgment,
or even effective opposition, must go further back
than this. The careful thinker will note that to some
degree the Klan is simply going beyond the rest of us
in dealing with ideas that are already held widely and
without offense—the idea that the country is suffering from too much unassimilated immigration and too
much bloc action by radical and religious groups, and
that attempts are being made to destroy the fundamental ideas of Americanism. He will remember,
too, that in spite of all the devastation and horror
they have caused many of the greatest forward movements of the world have been driven by these same
racial, patriotic and devout instincts and prejudices.
He will find sound judgment complicated.

To the average Klansman, however, the matter is
perfectly simple. With him the ideas are instinctive
and he trusts them. If you point out that they are
dangerous, he will reply that Christ declared He did
not come to bring peace to the world, but a sword.
He considers that this ends the argument.

The Klan leaders, in their defense, go far back of
this point—so far back that their attitude becomes one
not of defense but of attack. They deny that hatred
or injustice are involved in the lines they draw. On
the other hand they charge that while Protestant

natives have been liberal and have ignored race and religious lines, the members of other races and sects who have been allowed to share America's opportunities have held these lines tight and kept as many people as possible within the lines, have gained political, social and economic power for the groups thus formed, and have taken advantage of American good-nature to use that power against American natives and against the American tradition. In short, the Klan pleads both self-defense and extreme provocation.

Before taking up this plea in detail it is worth stopping a moment to look at the background of thought in the minds of "native, white, Protestant" Americans, to whom this attitude of the Klan appeals so powerfully and with such astounding success. In this background of thought are certain ideas which are so deep-rooted that they are actually instincts— subconscious and emotional. It contains prejudice but also patriotism, aspiration as well as fear, idealism, hatred, devotion, bitterness and self-sacrifice, all jumbled together in an almost unrecognizable mass. Usually, and perhaps wisely, it is complacently ignored, but now that the door has been opened it must be understood as far as possible, if the Klan itself, its power and its dangers are to be either understood or successfully combated, and if the issues the Klan has raised are to be met with any hope of a sound solution.

INVOKING THE WHIRLWIND

It is in this background of thought and feeling that the real strength of the Klan lies; in it one must seek to learn how powerful the Klan may become and how long it may last. It is there, too, and on the weighing of each of the many different elements involved, that the ultimate vindication or condemnation of the whole Klan movement will be found. Finally, it is there and only there that it can be fought, for the Klan idea *does* fit into this background, as its very success proves.

It is far beyond the scope of this book to go into the infinitely delicate questions of fact, feeling and instinct on which this background is based. That would involve all history, all philosophy and all psychology, at the very least. For the present purpose it is enough to point out in general terms the elements which are involved in the situation and a few facts about it. May I ask the reader to remember that in doing this I am merely reporting what I have found, neither approving nor condemning any part of it, and with a full realization that in so involved a subject my own observations can be no more than suggestive?

It must be recognized, first, that this background is there, however inarticulate it may be; ignoring it can only lead to misjudgment; denial of the real facts or ridicule of them makes things worse; suppression of the steam generated will increase the ultimate explosion. In the second place it is not all prejudice;

there is much sincere thought and there are some very real grievances. In the third place, there is a great difference in the emphasis placed by different individuals on the different elements involved; it must not be supposed that the whole of this half-subconscious feeling is equally effective with each man.

The largest single element is, undoubtedly, race prejudice, or race pride, or race instinct, as you prefer. It takes all forms from the high tradition of Nordic supremacy to the raw prejudice and contemptuous cruelty of the lowest order of toughs. It judges all other races as being lower in exact proportion as they differ from the Anglo-Saxon mixture which has become American, and it shows itself in pity or contempt according to the nature of each man. It produces lynchings, and a sincere and unselfish bearing of the "white man's burden" from the same box.

With the average run of Americans it is fairly expressed in the old army song about the Filipino:

"He may be a brother of William H. Taft's
But he ain't no friend of mine."

It is often curious in its manifestations, for I have seen a man, ruthless and brutal in his treatment of people who were not "white," respond finely to the appeal to "act like a white man." It is so deep that it is continually breaking out in queer and unconscious ways even in the very people who talk most of universal brotherhood. And, finally, it will not grow weaker in a country which uses "white" as the adjective of supreme praise for a man or an action.

Along with this goes national prejudice—or patriotism. This is based not only on a self-protective instinct, but also on a feeling that the country belongs by some right to the sons of the men who built it, and that newcomers should act as if they were here on sufferance. It runs against other breeds of the same race, though with less force, just as the race instinct runs against other races. It has in it much of contempt but more of fear; it includes a real pride in American achievements; a belief in American thought and ways; a jealousy of encroachment; it is, of course, much more than an instinct for it is fostered by our whole educational system and by the eloquence even of those who are trying to undermine it.

Both these instincts have been considerably badgered in America recently and are accordingly irritated; they re-act sharply against the alien who expresses his open contempt of American ways, who disregards them to his own profit, who makes himself too much at home in scoffing at American traditions, thought or feeling, or who, finally, undertakes to tell Americans how they ought to be, or think, or act. The justice of his criticism has nothing to do with the case. The average American is willing to be kind to the alien, but discounts all he may say in criticism of America on the ground that he is both self-interested and ignorant. Also, because he is exceeding his privileges. If the alien, by any shift, gets strength to put his ideas into effect, the American loses his good nature.

A final extreme irritant is the fact that so many speakers and editors consider anything American fair game for jibes or criticisms, from mannerisms of speech to the Puritan conscience, or the tradition of southern chivalry. The American can grin and bear it when these people make a by-word of "Americanism." But he does resent it when they shriek "persecution" and "prejudice" at any criticism of non-American people or thought.

The third of these instinctive hostilities is religious; specifically against the Roman Catholic Church, since the resentment against the Jew is far more racial than religious. The anti-Catholic feeling is based on the memory of three hundred years of war and persecution, on the belief that the Roman Church would if it dared and will if it ever does dare, renew both its persecution and its claim to political power, and the further belief that the Church does control the votes of most of its communicants. My own observation leads me to believe that it does not run so strongly against the Church itself as against the Knights of Columbus, who are considered the body through which it now applies political pressure.

It is hardly possible to exaggerate the strength of this feeling throughout the evangelical populations of the Middle West and the South. Men there may not be very active Protestants, but they are vigorously anti-Catholic. There is real fear in them. I know intelligent men, well educated, who were "brought up to believe"—and are not yet emotionally convinced to the contrary—that the day will come when they or their sons will have to fight with weapons in hand as their forefathers fought to escape Papal rule. The stories of guns buried under the churches are details; the fact is that they have a settled conviction that the Roman hierarchy still aims at world rule and will use any possible means to get it.

There are other elements in this background, which are, however, based more on reason. These grow out of wholly modern conditions, and need barely be mentioned—the evils arising from failure to assimilate recent immigration, the hyphenism which the war disclosed, the increasing tendency of all newcomers to unite against Americans instead of trying to become assimilated, the increasing solidarity of alien elements, and the rapid disappearance of the native American stock.

There have been recurrent outbreaks of this anti-American feeling since very early days. The most striking occurred in the early '30's in New York City, when Irish, German and other alien elements paraded under banners declaring "Americans Shall Not Rule Us." The recent outbreak—the "Revolt Against the Yankees"—has been almost as outspoken, having been consolidated by the European War. Excellent evidence of this revolt was furnished by the Wisconsin elections in 1922 when LaFollette so overwhelmingly carried the state. The reasons for his success were very frankly stated by Victor Berger who is always more outspoken than either LaFollette or the others of his alien-minded supporters. Berger's statement said in part:

"The United States are not an ethnical unit. Our population is of mixed European descent.

"Naturally, the inherited characteristics and instincts play a strong part in our lives, and even for that reason, alone, the American participation in the World War was a crime and a blunder. Our mission naturally should have been one of peace.

"Wisconsin is overwhelmingly German and Scandinavian.

"For some reason LaFollette always has had a strong hold on the Scandinavian farmers—which surely was not lessened by the position he took against the War, because the Scandinavians, by a large majority, were not in favor of the War.

"And undoubtedly LaFollette has gained the sympathies of ninety-nine per cent. of all the voters of German descent who by instinct as much as by political and economic insight were opposed to our entrance into the World War.

"Add to this that the Irish element during the War and since the War has also come to appreciate Robert M. LaFollette as he had never been appreciated before. It will be a sorry Irishman, indeed, who would vote for the Rev. 'Big Bill' Garfield in preference to voting for Robert M. LaFollette.

"The reactionaries in their stupidity have made the War the issue in this election. They have boldly proclaimed that the nomination and election of Robert M. LaFollette is to be considered a referendum on the War question.

"They will get their 'referendum.' "

These things are disturbing to all thinking, serious-minded men and women to-day, who it must be said are floundering in their search for cures. Their leadership, their thought are followed in cruder form by millions, and to these millions the Klan offers a solution of these particular and very real difficulties, as well as a vehicle for prejudice. Many of the men who oppose the Klan because they believe its methods dangerous or ineffective, nevertheless admit sympathy with its aims and have told me they believed the movement can only be stopped by curing these evils, or by the discovery of some better method of fighting them.

There is one more factor which is helping the Klan campaign. This is the wide-spread dissatisfaction among the farmers and moderately well-to-do, especially native Americans. Things are not going well with them, in ways other than economic; they see their children forced into occupations they detest, their schools invaded by teachers they distrust; their Sabbath sanctity violated, their laws broken almost with

105

impunity, and they, themselves, driven to meet competition by methods they abhor and to which they can not conscientiously adjust themselves. In other words, they are being forced to "change their ways."

They do not like it, and possibly would not even if the new ways were better. They do not enjoy having aliens pass them in prosperity, whether it is their own fault or due to the aliens' use of methods or of a standard of living which the American considers beneath him. Add to this race, national and religious prejudice and it is very easy for them to blame everything on the racial or religious alien. It is very easy for them to believe, too, that the alien is responsible for corruption in the cities, in business and in politics.

This is, in general terms, the background to which the Klan idea of "native, white, Protestant supremacy" appeals. These are the forces which it aims to gather together—which it actually is gathering together—for use in American political and social life. So the great charge, the most serious charge against the Klan is this—that it aims to use these forces by favoring native Protestants above all others, by discriminating against Jews, Catholics and Negroes, merely because they are Jews, Catholics and Negroes, and that in this way it is dividing the nation, cultivating hatred, developing class consciousness, and thus running flatly against the very structure of the democracy it is supposed to protect.

This accusation can not be better expressed than by

quoting from a recent speech of Senator Underwood:

"Under the ideals adopted by the fathers it (the American spirit) means that there shall be no discrimination against any citizen because of his belief," he said. "It does not mean that we will not drive a man from the street because he is of foreign birth, but that when he is adopted into the fold of American citizenship he stands on his own feet, the peer of any other citizen. These are the principles of this country. Tear them down and you tear the flag down with them."

One more thing should perhaps be said about the background of American thought, in reference to this matter of principles. The Klan denies that Underwood states the case correctly—denies that a man is entitled to be treated as an American unless he acts like one. But aside from this, the appeal "on principle" will have little influence on the kind of average citizens to whom the Klan appeals. The American breed is, when all is said and done, a rather lawless one in emergencies. It is sentimental. It is also practical. Its slogans and to a large extent its principles have been adopted because they are or were useful. It is an historical fact that it has never applied those slogans or principles when they caused much inconvenience. Equality, freedom, free speech, even legal safeguards, have been thrown overboard time and again—and the jettisoning justified satisfactorily—when they failed to produce the results wanted.

The same thing is true in regard to any meticulous observance of law. We Americans prefer to let the law do things for us just so long as it does the things we want, but the principle of lawfulness is far less important to us than the idea of getting those things done somehow. We have the curious habit of making laws for other people rather than for ourselves, and we break laws so continually that it seems almost as if we reserved the right to do so whenever we feel disposed. The Klan is, therefore, entirely in harmony with American character when it stresses the things it wants to accomplish and is impatient when fault is found with its methods.

Consider for example two instances, neither important in itself, but each illustrating how the American mind works in regard to law enforcement. The first shows how usual it is for us to demand that everybody obey the laws which we personally approve, and yet how we personally refuse to obey the laws we do not approve.

In the town of Ludington, Michigan, a group of reformers last fall set out to put a stop to Sunday dancing. They pointed out quite truthfully that the law forbade Sunday dancing. They neglected to point out that Sunday newspapers, movies, soda fountains, golf, tennis and automobiling were also forbidden. The prosecutor announced that he would enforce the

INVOKING THE WHIRLWIND

Sunday laws—all the laws. The people rose in their might; even the leaders of reform objected to this "narrow legalistic view" and complained bitterly because of the prosecutor's "petty persecution for technical violations." Eventually none of the laws were enforced!

The second illustration is in a way more important. It also shows a national instinct, an instinct to use private justice when we feel so moved. It is a story which may or may not be true about an interview between Roosevelt and the Kaiser. His Imperial Majesty pointed out to the ex-President that he had some 2,000,000 friends of Germany in this country who, he declared, would prevent America from taking any attitude hostile to German ambitions.

"Oh, no, Your Majesty," said Roosevelt. "They wouldn't do that. We have a good many more than 2,000,000 lamp posts in America, and lots of rope."

Now it is clear that this story is an indictment of the whole American nation, intimating that we are all ready to go in for a national lynching bee if sufficiently provoked. I suppose no one would defend the idea that we should hang even disloyal Germans to our lamp posts, as a common practise. Yet this story is credited to one of the greatest and best of Americans, and certainly one typical of our best. It may not be true, but it sounds very much like him.

I have told this story to many people, including some of the most rarefied-minded intellectuals. There has not been one American of the lot who has not responded with a whole-hearted laugh. Some men of other breeds have been greatly distressed over the lack of moral sensitiveness implied, but the Americans seem to approve the sentiment implied.

There can be little doubt that the story is a true parable and that in an emergency Americans will enforce their own law—not merely their statutes but also fundamental laws that they believe essential for their own or the national good—and that they will use lamp posts if it should become necessary. This has been proved over and over again, not only by the hideous record of lynchings and by the daily appearance of the unwritten law in our courts, but by the vigilance committees, by the present highly respectable defiance of the Volstead Act, and in a thousand other ways. Such things have been common throughout our history; they are common to-day.

Another point about the "Klan's violation of American principles": there is no warrant in history for believing that Americans have ever worried very much about the freedom of any one but themselves. Certainly our Puritan ancestors, who contributed a very considerable share to the American idea, did not do so. They came to this country because they wished to worship in their own way, and they immediately took pains to see that nobody else should worship in any other way. Also they enacted the most rigid blue laws, calling for the most intolerable interference with freedom of private conduct that can well be imagined. Some of the things for which the Klan is most vigorously criticized are entirely in harmony with New England traditions.

Taking all these things into consideration, and assuming that what America has done once it is quite likely to do again in similar circumstances, there can be little surprise either at the Klan's narrowness, or at its occasional lawlessness. It is certainly quite typical for a body of Americans suffering under irritation to take any means that seem likely to relieve it, letting theories, principles and legality go hang until some more convenient season. There is even reason to believe that the present Klan movement has in some respects acted as a safety valve for discontent, which, if it had been restrained too long, might have broken out in some far more dangerous and destructive way.

Since these things are true the conclusion is inevitable; that the only effective way to check the Klan movement is to go back into the prejudices or instincts on which it depends, and to show Klansmen that these basic ideas are wrong in themselves or—what would be easier though far from easy—to show that it is not necessary to call them into action now.

An eminently practical attitude is expressed very clearly in the reply Dr. Evans, the Imperial Wizard, made when I put these charges to him. His answer also disclosed another attitude, the curious assumption that people coming to America expect, or at any rate are expected, to approve and adopt traditional American ism, instead of trying to change America to their own taste. His answer ignores the fact that every other race, nationality or religion has traditions as instinctive to it as the American spirit is to Americans; and that they can not possibly leave these traditions at Ellis Island, even if they wished to. But to this, also, the Klan has an answer; it would bar all such aliens until or unless they really want to become Americans.

"No matter what your intentions are," I had told Dr. Evans, "the fact is that the Klan is not bringing love and brotherhood into the country. It is causing sharper divisions, and instead of breaking up the alien groups, is driving them together."

"Quite likely," he responded. "The Klan is standing in the way of the selfish interests and purposes of these groups, and naturally they are increasing their efforts. They were having things pretty much their own way before, and didn't have to work very hard to get what they wanted. The Klan merely acts according to the facts. The whole country recognizes that there are millions of un-American citizens, that they are not being assimilated, and that many of them can not be assimilated. Every publication and public man has been talking about it for years. Every one admits that the security of the country is in danger. But no one does anything.

"The Klan does do something. It sets up, in the

first place, a standard of Americanism. If we find it is wrong we can change it—at any rate there it is. We invite every man or woman (except Negroes, who are a special case) to meet that standard, and they all could do it. We propose means to help them meet it. We propose means to keep the evil from growing worse. And we propose also that people who do not meet it shall have full liberty, but they shall not be given a chance to corrupt and destroy our government and our institutions.

"It is our Christian duty to love our enemies, but not to let them destroy us. It is also our Christian duty to fight evil, and no sensible man will deny that unassimilated and unpatriotic elements in our population are an evil and a tremendous one."

"But has not the Klan gathered much strength by appealing to distinctly anti-social race and religious prejudices?" I demanded.

"That is one of the evils we are trying to correct," he replied. "The Klan to-day does not deal in hatred, or cultivate division between races or religions. It specifically declines any applicant who wishes to join for that reason, if his intentions are learned. The most that can be said is that it recognizes the distinctions as to race and religious divisions which actually exist.

"Many other organizations have specific restrictions on membership, and the restrictions in the Klan naturally call forth the implication of your question. I believe that many people have joined this movement from unworthy motives, because such an institution seems to them to give opportunity for gratification of selfish purposes. But no institution can protect itself against such people until their motives are made clear by action. One of the remarkable things about the Klan is the ability and thoroughness with which it cleanses itself from within."

"But does not the Klan, by drawing these distinctions, tend to solidify these classes and therefore to prevent Americanizing them, and thus defeat its own aims?" I insisted.

"The Klan is opposed to class distinction of any kind or to political action or social action on any other basis than that of pure Americanism," he declared. "However, the fact is that these classes exist and are active politically, socially and economically as groups and classes. This is recognized by every politician. Americans, so long as they are unorganized, are helpless before the demands and attacks of these groups. So long as they remain it is necessary for the protection of America that Americans themselves appear and act together. In the long run the doctrine of love, Americanism and awakened consciousness will draw these classes together and away from the false ideas that cause these barriers."

Without disparaging Dr. Evans' oratory, it seemed to me that the most effective answer to the criticisms of the Klan's exclusive membership, and to the race and religious distinctions it draws, came from a well-known artist.

"Rot!" he said when the criticisms were made. "I wouldn't be allowed to join the Knights of Columbus or B'nai Brith. Why in Hades should their members object if I join an order that bars them out?"

"But the Klan is a political body, with very definite aims," I objected. "Those others aren't."

"More rot!" he exploded. "You don't believe that yourself. If they haven't got definite aims and aren't in politics, then I'm a Chinaman."

These, then, seem to be the important facts about the Klan's "campaign of hate." It does, beyond question, appeal to deep, powerful, explosive race and religious instincts and prejudices; ideas which are hideously dangerous or heroically valuable, according to how they are put in action. It does also attempt to offer a solution for the grave national problems which race and religion produce, to which we are so sensitive that they are usually ignored, but which are causing deep concern to all thinking Americans. It does, officially at least, attempt to solve those problems without using the prejudices and hatred which are the almost inevitable results of bringing those questions into the open. And it is in just this field that it finds its greatest strength, and presents its gravest danger.

CHAPTER VI

THE BUSINESS OF "KLUXING"

THOUGH the sins of the Klan be as scarlet, yet the world will always owe it a little something for giving us the verb "to klux," with its derivatives "kluxing" and "kluxer." They enrich the language. We have long needed some word to express the vociferous rounding up of the populace which is one of our great national activities. "Kluxing" does it to a nicety; not merely because of the barnyard suggestion in the sound of the word but because of its brevity, its implied humor, its onomatopœic fitness. It ought to come into wide use very rapidly.

The Ku Klux Klan has brought recruiting to a point of efficiency which is almost scientifically perfect and far beyond any similar system. No matter how much credit is given to the appeal made by its ideals and purposes, these could not propagate themselves. It is great skill in kluxing that has spread them so far and so fast.

Much of the Klan propaganda needs very little mention as it is entirely in harmony with the ideals and professions already reported. In the addresses of its leading speakers and in the columns of the publications controlled by its national officers, one finds much that is fine and stimulating and little that can be construed as an appeal to hatred even by the most bitter critic. Its proposals and assumptions are of course debatable, the foundation of "native, white, Protestant supremacy" is always present, but within those bounds the appeal is to the best side of patriotism and religious devotion and there is no inconsistency and no sign of hypocrisy. It would seem that the effect of this form of propaganda must be on the whole stimulating and inspiring. It is far below abstract idealism, but almost as far above average thought and practise.

But this is only one side of the Klan appeal. There is another side which fosters and stimulates tremendous evils. In fact, in turning from the theory and ideals of the Klan, with which we have so far been concerned, to its actual operation, we find these evils in every field. The practises of Klans and individual Klansmen fall far short of the professions made; faults appear of which there is no hint in the platforms; there are discrepancies so great that it is very easy to discredit all talk of ideals and high aims as the merest camouflage.

This verdict would be unavoidable if it were not that the evidences of high aims and idealism do also appear. The same thing is true in some degree of every organization, since all organizations come far short of carrying out their ideals—there are many men who quite sincerely condemn every church and every other idealistic body on just these grounds. The Klan is at least as fallible in its workings as are the churches!

Judgment will largely depend, in the end, on the point of view. It is possible to think of the Klan as actually an idealistic—if often mistaken—body, struggling to maintain its high aims against the faults and mistakes and selfishness and sometimes downright criminality of its agents and members, and wrestling with the compromises which must be made by any organization if it is to gain the strength for effective action. There are always such compromises; a recent similar case was that of Roosevelt, who in organizing his Progressive Party used many discredited politicians, the riff-raff, the down-and-outers and the "lunatic fringe." The Klan has all these elements in it.

It is just as easy, because of these same facts, to decide that the Klan's professions are purely hypocritical, that its hidden purposes are as evil as imagination can conceive, that the real control lies with the most vicious elements, that all its decent actions are dust thrown in the eyes of opinion, and that it is only in its worst deeds that it has dared to drop its disguise and act as it really desires and as it would act everywhere if it dared. This belief is of course very common; it seems to have about the same degree of reason as the anti-Catholic belief mentioned in the last chapter—that the Catholic Church will resume burning Protestants at the stake whenever it dares. The fact seems to be that the Klan, like every other body, has both idealists and materialists, saints and sinners and that there is always struggle between them.

It is certain that, just as the Klan appears at its best when talking of ideals and purposes, it appears at its worst in its day-to-day workings. The compromises or revelations, mistakes or vices—you can take your choice—which show in actual operation are far below its own standards.

Furthest below of all, perhaps, is its work of recruiting—its kluxing. Recruiting seems to be a business which always brings out the worst in any man or organization, since it is so easy to believe that almost any kind of support is worth gaining for the sake of "the larger cause," and that almost any means of winning recruits is justified, also by that cause. I know one utterly devoted head of a missionary college who has sold his soul to perdition if half the stories told of his lies and subterfuges in enlisting workers, are true! I have rarely known of a leader in any cause who refused support, however vicious, if only it would actually work for the object he aimed at. Since this is true of admittedly great movements, and of splendid leaders, the Klan can hardly be expected to do better.

As to the means used to get recruits, any one can

recall many instances of methods quite on a par with those of the Ku Klux Klan which have been used with general popular approval and have been backed by very high-class men. There is, for instance, the system of selling insurance by trying to scare the prospect with lugubrious fiction regarding the horrid fates of the wives and daughters of men who left no estate; there is the evangelism which attempts to save souls through stirring up emotion by hypnotic processes, by threats of hell-fire and by a pathos that would be too raw for the pages of the yellowest journals, and finally, there was the recent war propaganda, paid for from government funds, by which we were all officially, systematically and impudently lied to. In view of these facts it is clear that there are considerable classes who are barred from criticizing the Klan recruiting methods.

One qualification should be made, not only as to this report on the Klan's recruiting methods, but as to all my reports on its actual workings. It is possible to say that certain good or bad things have been done by the Klan, but it is not possible to say how much there has been of each, or to strike an average of conduct. In a body of such size and such secrecy nothing less than omniscience can determine on which side the balance stands, for no matter how much is learned there will always be much that can not be discovered. I do not believe that the leaders themselves know these things with any accuracy.

THE BUSINESS OF "KLUXING"

I can only say this—and I realize that it has too little weight to determine even my own opinion—that so far as my own observations go, and in spite of the confusing mixture of good and bad in many things, the useful actions of the Klan seem on the whole to outnumber the harmful, and the general level of Klan activity seems to be improving considerably.

This, of course, is outside any question of the good or evil in the Klan movement itself. And also it is aside from the fact that the Klan can not escape responsibility for the evils which exist, or at least escape the burden of proof of lack of responsibility, since it uses an organization and a type of propaganda which make those evils easy.

The kluxing system of the Klan was invented by Edward Young Clark, the man whose huge profit was one of the main targets in the Congressional inquiry two years ago, whose departure from the Klan was accelerated when Dr. Evans and the reform group took charge, who recently offered to help President Coolidge expose the organization and is now promoting a rival Klan. The system's simple efficiency stamps him as almost a genius.

At the head of the kluxers is the Imperial Wizard; each state is in charge of a King Kleagle who employs the Field Kleagles. The details vary, but as a rule these Field Kleagles get $4.00 a head for every member enrolled; the King Kleagles get $2.00 a head, and the balance of the $10.00 initiation fee goes to the Imperial Treasury. Expenses must always be paid by each officer or agent from his own share of the fees. The Imperial Government supplies high-grade speakers in large number, paying their salaries. The King Kleagles pay the expenses of the speakers in their territories, the salaries and expenses of minor speakers, officers and office workers and organization in general; the field men pay their own costs, including lecture halls. The whole army is spurred on and trained by special instructors, paid from national headquarters and working along the lines of any modern selling organization.

The commission system is, naturally, immensely effective, far more than any straight salaries scheme. It keeps each Field Kleagle on his toes every minute, stimulates his salesmanship and ingenuity to the utmost, eliminates unsuccessful men promptly and leaves no room for discord. It has resulted in what seems the best selling organization in America.

From its very nature, however, the system has its great faults. One is the chance that some of the Kleagles will make enormous profits, that the whole thing will appear as a profit-making scheme, mulcting the "suckers" of their $10.00 "klectokon" and providing comfortable living for a large number of loafers. This is at least half true, but then every organized movement is more or less open to the same charges; has its abuses, wastes money, and many overpay its officers and collectors. It is very easy for opponents to believe that these expenses and wastes are so great that they may fairly be called graft, and that the backers of such organizations are actually working for their own pockets rather than for the charity. Similar charges are made against the Y. M. C. A., Anti-Saloon League, Charity Organization Society, Salvation Army—everything!

The actual profits of the Kleagles do not seem to be very large. Klansmen tell of three or four who have made $50,000 a year by unusually successful campaigns, but the average earning is said to be under $5,000. I can not, of course, guarantee these figures, but they check up fairly well with what I have been able to learn of the number of enrollments. This does not show unusually high pay for good salesmanship.

The total amount gathered by Klan organizers in the last year is staggering, however. On the basis of three million initiations it would be $30,000,000, but Kleagles often accept notes for a portion of the initiation fee so that this must be discounted somewhat. There should be added, however, the dues of fifteen cents a month, which each Klansman pays into the various treasuries; a total of more than $8,000,000 a year. Most of this stops in the hands of the Field Kleagles and goes for necessary expenses. It seems safe on the whole to estimate that the Klan expenditure for propagation in the last year has not been less than $25,000,000, and may have reached

$35,000,000. With such funds it is no wonder that the Klan grows rapidly.

A far more serious fault than high pay for organizers is the pressure which this system puts on Kleagles to take in every member they can get and to use every kind of an argument or appeal that they think may work. Apparently they do. I have not learned of a single case where a Kleagle refused a member—who had $10.00—no matter how vicious or dangerous he might be. And there are reports, wherever the Klan organizers are active, of the use of the most abominable forms of appeal.

The worst of these I have heard of in three different places, but always at second hand, so I can not say definitely that it has come from Klan organizers, but only that it has come from Klan members. It is an argument said to be offered to prospective members who hesitate. This is it: "If you have any doubt about the ability of the Klan to enforce its orders, or to protect its members, look at what we got away with at Mer Rouge."

Now, every high official of the Klan with whom I have talked denies flatly that Klansmen were guilty of any murders at Mer Rouge. They also deny, as has been said over and over again, that the Klan countenances or protects lawlessness of any kind. I reported this Mer Rouge statement to Dr. Evans.

"That is either the statement of an enemy of the Klan within the organization, or of a badly misguided

Kleagle," he said. "If such a statement is made by a Kleagle, a report of it will reach headquarters very shortly, and will result not only in the Kleagle's prompt dismissal, but in his banishment from the organization."

I may add that in the one case I was able to check up, this was done. In every case I have known of, when such conditions were reported to headquarters, prompt action was taken. But the system itself stimulates just such abuses. It is needless to point out that they give the lie to every ideal the Klan professes.

Dr. Evans believes that all these kluxing evils carry their own corrective. He says:

"This is a matter that has been a problem to all executives, and even to-day there is debate as to the better form—straight commission, salary and commission or salary only. Possibly the present system has a tendency to make Kleagles accept undesirable individuals. But it has been our experience thus far in the new order of things, that Kleagles very quickly learn that the successful development of a particular unit of organization depends on the high class of the individuals that form the nucleus around which they build. Many of them have found, much to their regret, that they have inadvertently let an undesirable individual slip in. Immediately they have found a slowing up in their organization work and sometimes we have had to send other Kleagles to investigate before we have found the cause.

"The experience with the Kleagles has been—and this is quite true—that they guard the membership very closely, realizing that undesirable individuals retard propagation. Therefore the commission system really does not bring about the condition that might generally be expected to follow. Further, the surest way for a Kleagle to make certain of his discharge would be to admit an unworthy man or to spread propaganda not in harmony with the principles of the organization."

There is undoubtedly some truth in this, but it fails to cover two cases: First, places where the general tone of a community is so low that the profits will be greater if the lower elements instead of the better are organized, and second, cases where a few extra dollars can be made by slipping in undesirables after the organization is well started. The evidence which has come to me indicates that Kleagles sometimes have made profits by debasing the Klan propaganda to meet and take advantage of both these situations; that a considerable number of vicious types is admitted and that in some communities the Klan is composed almost entirely of the lower elements.

As previously stated, I can not give the average condition, though it does seem to be improving, and is much better in the states where the Klan is comparatively new. I believe the earlier propaganda was largely responsible for the various evils and that Dr. Evans and his supporters are trying to remove them.

126

THE BUSINESS OF "KL JXING"

The propaganda of the Klan (as distinct from the kluxing) takes three main forms. First is that of the speakers. Such speeches as I have heard or on which I have full reports, are open to very little criticism. They follow the lines of the Klan appeal already reported—better government, better citizenship, patriotism and religion in general, and "native, white, Protestant supremacy." They have been fine, spirited, balanced, eloquent, without any attempt to stir prejudice or appeal to hatred except that which comes from the subject itself. They are as good, or as bad, as the Klan movement at its best.

A typical speech was one given early in the fall of 1923, in northern Ohio. The speaker was not introduced nor identified in any way. A careful watch was kept for improper remarks, but except for an occasional reference to "a white man's country" none was found. He spoke eloquently of the evils in the country, the weaknesses of the government, the decay of public morality, the prevalence of business fraud, the possibilities of legal injustice, the need of better education, and the importance of national unity. He urged his audience as men, Americans and Christians to forget differences and selfish interests and to unite to make a better nation, safer homes. The entire address was sound, sensible, appealing—and effective. It was a mixture of patriotism and religion without mixing church and state. It might have been made by a first-class evangelist or a truly patriotic politician.

The published propaganda—the Klan press—is far different, however. There are printed some thirty Klan papers, with a combined circulation of more than a million and a half—another testimonial to the strength of the movement. The style of most of these publications is execrable, but perhaps no worse than the worst of country weeklies. They print much the same matter, though they add pleas for Christian and patriotic idealism of about the intellectual level of a yellow editorial, but in support of Klan doctrine.

In addition, however, almost all of them carry definite appeals to hatred and prejudice; usually against the Catholics. This is crude, raw, sometimes indecent. A few samples will illustrate.

The Protestant Standard, of Merryville, Louisiana, carries these head-lines: "Klan Calls Rome's Hand in Oklahoma. Jesuit Judases Jeopardize American Life and Liberty. Pope Uses Walton in Effort to Bring Back Inquisition of Dark Ages." The text under these heads shows that Walton is having the Klan investigated by courts martial.

The Good Citizen, of Zerepath, New Jersey, says in its editorial on "The Rising of the Ku Klux Klan: . . . now Rome has come across the great sea with her un-American hordes, to sweep away Protestantism as with a flood. For a time she was restrained, but she grows bolder in her assaults on Protestant institutions, in her efforts to make this country subserve the purposes of the Vatican.'

THE BUSINESS OF "KLUXING"

The Patriot, published in St. Louis, tells how "Syracuse, New York, Patriots Rally to Defend Public Schools from Rome-Controlled Politicians."

The Arkansas Traveller, of Little Rock, prints under the caption of "Lincoln's Warning" a statement beginning: "I do not pretend to be a prophet, I see a very dark cloud on our horizon. That dark cloud is coming from Rome. . . . A cyclone such as the world has never seen will pass over the country, spreading ruin and desolation from north to south." There is nothing to show that "Lincoln" said this, or where.

The Texas 100 Per Cent American under the heading

"LIES—LIES—LIES"

editorially addresses a priest who had written to *The Outlook* in defense of the Catholic Church, and says:

"Now, Reverend Sir, you who wears his collar backward like a mule, that you have denied that the Jesuit Order or the entire Catholic world for that matter, does not hold to the doctrine that the end justifies the means, we should like for you to deny some other things.

Did Your Church Cremate Joan of Arc?

129

THE CHALLENGE OF THE KLAN

"Was Joan of Arc burned as a heretic by your fanatical followers, or rather those who led your church in the centuries past?

"Deny that if you can.

"Then, after she had been burned at the stake for being heretical, why did your church in these latter days canonize her?

"Come on, Rome, we are asking you!"

Following are a half dozen other quotations from the rabid Klan press illustrating the frequency of the appeal to religious hatred:

"Charleston, South Carolina.—The plan of Governor Walton, of Oklahoma, to secure the assistance of the Knights of Columbus organization through the wholesale enlistment of its members in the state militia, as was stated in a dispatch from Chicago last week, is to be supplemented by financial aid from the same source. The Liberty Boys and Belles of this city, an organization affiliated with the Knights of Columbus, has instructed its secretary to notify the 'mad governor of Oklahoma' that 'we are eager to help you financially in our humble way and stand ready to call upon all true Americans everywhere to join in the fund to carry on the fight. How may

130

we proceed under your sanction, properly safeguarding every dollar until it is used for its noble purpose?'

"Although the inquiry regarding the proper safeguarding of the funds of Governor Walton implies somewhat of a suspicion in the minds of Governor Walton's Roman Catholic friends that the money sent to him may not be properly used, it is presumed that hatred for the Klan will offset any doubt of the governor's financial integrity and that the 'Liberty Boys and Belles' will take the chance." (From *The Fellowship Forum, Washington,* District of Columbia.)

"New York City—Romanism, the wet forces, bootleggers, and all the anti-American elements which so largely predominate in this city were startled last Saturday night at the exhibition of strength which the Ku Klux Klan gave at an initiation ceremony in which 500 candidates were naturalized." (From *The Fellowship Forum,* Washington, District of Columbia.)

INVISIBLE EMPIRE TO WATCH IS NOT THE KLAN

"The nine men arrested on the charge of inciting to riot in connection with the Carnegie, Pennsylvania,

131

mob affair, in which one Klansman was killed and a number of others seriously injured, have been freed of all responsibility in the matter. What happened to be a plain case of murder on the night of August 25 quickly resolved itself into the insignificant charge of 'inciting to riot.'

"The Roman Catholic undertaker, McDermott, whom four witnesses, it was stated in the newspaper account the morning following the murder, saw fire four or five shots directly at the murdered Klansman Abbott, was not even called upon to answer to the charge of murder.

"While Roman Catholics are glibly prating of the invisible empire of the Ku Klux Klan, their own 'invisible empire' of the Jesuits steadily pursues its goal to 'make America Catholic.' The means to be employed matters not. Protecting murderers, bootleggers and backing up the mad governor of Oklahoma is all in a day's work of this 'invisible' organization.

"And yet there are some Masons who would help persecute and prosecute the Klan and thus become the subservient tool of the 'invisible empire' of Rome. In the light of daily events transpiring, showing the mysterious, powerful influence which controls the courts wherever Roman Catholicism and its subjects are concerned, it would seem the 'invisible empire' of the Jesuits is the organization that requires the careful scrutiny of patriotic Americans, rather than the Klan, which stands for the same principles and the ideals

132

THE BUSINESS OF "KLUXING"

espoused by Freemasons." (From *The Fellowship Forum*, Washington, District of Columbia.)

THE RISING OF THE KU KLUX KLAN—THE NEW REFORMATION

"On account of the abuses of religion by the Roman Catholic hierarchy, civilization had reached a universal crisis in the sixteenth century; and Martin Luther, the chosen instrument of God, was placed in the breach to prevent the wheels of progress from being reversed and the world from being plunged into greater darkness than that of the Dark Ages.

"The thousand years preceding the Reformation, known by religious historians as Satan's Millennium, was brought on by the Romish Church with her paganistic worship and practices, during which time millions of men and women poured out their blood as martyrs of the Christian religion. . . .

THE WHITE-ROBED ARMY

"Now come the Knights of the Ku Klux Klan in this crucial hour of our American history to contend for the faith of our fathers who suffered and died in behalf of freedom. At the psychological moment

133

they have arrived to encourage the hearts of those who have been battling heroically for the rights and privileges granted them under the Constitution of the United States.

"How our hearts have been thrilled at the sight of this army! Words fail to express the emotions of the soul at the appearance of this mighty throng upon the battle-field, where a few faithful followers of the lowly Nazarene have been contending for the faith once delivered to the Saints, against Papal mobs who have torn down gospel tabernacles, wrecked buildings and imprisoned Protestant worshipers.

OUR NATIONAL PERIL

"The World War was the signal for greater alarm than the average American has been willing to admit. Notwithstanding the sacrifices that had to be made at home and the thousands of our young men who crossed the sea and laid down their lives on the battle-fields of the Old World, it has taken the Ku Klux Klan to awaken even a portion of the population of the United States to our national peril. Our religious and political foes are not only within our gates, but are coming by the hundreds of thousands, bringing the chaos and ruin of old European and Asiatic countries to un-Americanize and destroy our nation, and to make it subserve the purposes of the Pope in his aspirations for world supremacy.

134

THE BUSINESS OF "KLUXING"

ROME WOULD OVERTHROW PUBLIC SCHOOLS

"One of the great efforts of the Roman hierarchy toward this end is to get control of our public schools by placing Roman Catholics on school boards and in the schoolrooms and taking the Bible out of the schools. In the event of their success in their efforts to overthrow our present school system there would be a string of beads around every Protestant child's neck and a Roman Catholic catechism in his hand. 'Hail Mary, Mother of God,' would be on every child's lips, and the idolatrous worship of dead saints a part of the daily programme.

THE JEWISH AND CATHOLIC ALLIANCE

"The money-grasping Jew, who has no use for the Christ of Calvary, does all in his power to bring discredit on Christianity, and would be pleased to see the whole structure broken down, and in this way get rid of his responsibility for crucifying the Christ on Calvary and bringing the curse on his race, which they have had to suffer since the beginning of the Christian era. The sons of Abraham have therefore become a strong ally to the Papacy, not because they have anything in common with it in religion, but in

135

their political propaganda against American institutions and principles.

"While no true Christian has anything against the Jew, it must be admitted that this alliance with the Papacy is a dangerous menace to our flag and country. The Jew is insoluble and indigestible; and when he grows in numbers and power till he becomes a menace to Christianity and the whole moral fabric, drastic measures will have to be taken to counteract his detructive work,, and more especially when he is in alliance with the old Papal religio-political machine." (From *The Good Citizen,* Zarephath, New Jersey.)

AWAKE! AMERICANS, AWAKE!

"Awake, Americans! You descendants of the patriots of the Revolution! You sons of the Pilgrim Fathers who fought back the hordes of the Tyrant! Gird on the armor of God who led you out of bondage and chased slavery from out of our land! There is an enemy without our gates ten thousand times more dangerous than the redcoats ever were!

"Catholic politicians are filling the air with propaganda which would lead you to believe that old Ship of State has broken loose from her moorings and is drifting far to sea. They cry out in tones of agony that people are growing intolerant and Protestants are

136

seeking to abridge religious liberty. Catholics will prescribe our religion and forbid a Protestant funeral in a Catholic Church. Forbid Catholics attendance at Masonic funerals and then lay claim to a corner on tolerance. Now when Rome is caught red handed in her designs to make American Catholics and Protestants interfere, she cries intolerance and would have you believe that liberty is crushed and bleeding.

"When Protestants exercise a right guaranteed to all under the Constitution, when Americans meet in peaceable assembly, Catholics arm themselves with bludgeons and blunderbusses and try to beat down honest men and murder American citizens. Only fools resort to force to settle a dispute and bricks and rocks are only used by savages. Rome not having any grounds on which to fight in the realm of reason seeks to unite State and Church by the use of sandbags and billies. Reason and enlightenment with them are taboo. Blind passion is appealed to and ignorance is made a virtue. Intellectual darkness for the masses is sought by Rome as surely as a robber seek the shadows. For when the bright light of reason shines upon her, priests lose their power, and her influence crumbles as hastily as would a snowbank in the nether regions.

"Catholic politicians, if intrusted with power, would pass laws to force American organizations out of existence and shackle liberty, as they have done in every clime wherein they have reigned supreme.

137

THE CHALLENGE OF THE KLAN

"There are men seeking high office in Louisiana to-day who if elected in numbers sufficient would jail Americans for assembling in peaceful meetings and give to Rome the revenue of our State. Take the Eagle from off the dollar and in its stead place a likeness of the unholy face of Pius. Strip the stripes from the American Flag and rend the Stars asunder, and make for us a National banner with background dark and gloomy, and mount upon it a cluster of garlic to commemorate the odor that permeates the Vatican. Turn back the march of civilization and chain the Bible to a box. Tether the intellects of man and enslave reason. Place a statue of a priest where now stands the Goddess of Liberty and place in his hand the torch of intolerance. Demolish our free institutions of learning and imprison those bold enough to preach freedom of the masses. Have black-robed nuns who know only slavery teach our children and drown our art in miasmic ignorance.

"Not all Catholics are of this stripe, but those who seek high office are tainted woefully with Catholic teachings and some have been so bold as to proclaim no Protestant is fit for office and Catholics are the only hope of liberty.

"Yes, we have no bananas." (From *The Protestant Standard*, Merryville, Louisiana.)

138

THE BUSINESS OF "KLUXING"

AMERICANS ATTENTION

The American Free Public School is the Foundation of our Free Institutions

---

ROME HATES PUBLIC SCHOOLS

" 'Education must be controlled by Catholic authorities, even to war and bloodshed.'—*The Catholic World*.

" 'Education outside the Catholic church is a damnable heresy.'—Pope Piux IX.

" 'We must take part in the elections, move in solid mass against the old party pledged to sustain the integrity of the public schools.'—Cardinal McCluskey.

" 'The public schools have produced nothing but a Godless generation of thieves and blackguards.'—Father Shaner.

" 'The common schools of this country are sinks of moral pollution and nurseries of hell.'—*The Chicago Tablet*.

" 'I frankly confess that the Catholics stand before

139

the country as the enemies of the public schools.'—
Father Phelan.

"No American opposes American schools!"—
(From *The Patriot*, St. Louis, Missouri.)

————

ALKALI IKE, ALCOHOL AL

"Have you ever heard of Alkali Ike? Ike was a
bad egg who could put down more Arizona rotgut,
and brag about more killings that he never did, than
any rattlesnake of a two-gun fighter who ever in-
fested the cactus-dotted western plains. Ike was a
rip roarin' snorter, and to hear him tell it, he was
the originator of the private graveyard idea. Ike has
bloomed, and Ike has prospered, but Ike is now forgotten, because a greater than Ike has come to usurp
Ike's place in the sun.

ALCOHOL AL

"Alcohol Al, is the name of the newcomer. Once-
uponatime there was a fish peddler in New York,
and peddling fish among the homes of the Tammany
politicians and ward heelers, he soon learned that it
was easier to shoot suckers than it was to shoot fish.
Accordingly, like all second-story workers he joined

the second-story workers' union, which in New York is known by the name of Itstammanyhall. In due process of time Tammany jimmied Al into a political job, but not until they had sent his history, photograph and autograph, and his confession made to a priest, to the little papa in Rome, and asked him to approve. The little papa approved with a flourish and a big proviso. The flourish carried his signature and the seal of the Vatican, and the proviso was that some day Alcohol Al should kiss the Papal toe, as all good Catholic brethren had done, who had before been passed to occupy political office in the United States of America.

GOVERNOR

"Finally after repeated approvals of the Pope on Al, as he moved from political office to political office, his political owners, the Pope—and Tammany Hall—decided that they would put him in the office of Governor of the State. . . .

" . . . once let either the Republicans or the Democrats do so foul a thing as to try to offer for suffrage that flagrant defier of American laws, Alcohol Al Smith, for the presidency or the vice-presidency, and the match is to the tinder, and nothing short of heaven can stop the movement until the new-born American

party shall have placed its candidates at the head of
the nation.

THAT IS IN THE CARDS

"The Texas American has been preaching *'Why
not a Klansman for the presidency?'* It may not come
to that exactly in our next presidential campaign, but
it is written in the cards that none but a 100 per cent
American shall be our next President.

"Choose ye Democrats, choose ye Republicans, this
day. Whom will ye serve? Do you intend to flaunt
in the faces of your former constituents, the same
old things that have been in the past? Do ye intend
to temporize with the Roman Catholic hierarchy? Do
you intend to let any set of men, who are greatly in
the minority, compel you to betray the American
people?

"It can't be done. You can't get away with it this
time. There is entirely too much political independ-
ence for any set of men to drag this country's fair
name in the mud any longer.

"The people are going to name, and the people are
going to elect the next president of the United States,
and it will not be Alcohol Al Smith of New York,
nor any other defier of the Constitution, but it will be
an American through and through. This is a Protestant Christian Nation." (From *The Texas 100 Per
Cent American,* Dallas, Texas.)

THE BUSINESS OF "KLUXING"

There is any quantity of such stuff. It reminds one somewhat of the propaganda of the Know-nothings though it is far milder, for they filled the country with supposed confessions of monks and nuns, with sickeningly illustrated brochures on the inquisition and on martyrdom, and similar horrors. This lessened virulence is probably encouraging, but the stuff is more than bad enough.

There is, however, a good deal of material that is just as definitely—perhaps even more definitely, and certainly with more approval from high Klan officials —Klan propaganda which is harmless and some of which has a definite tendency to promote good citizenship. Some examples of this, part of them from the same organs already quoted, follow:

"Can't hate. No, you can't, Klansmen. You know that is not part of the Klan Creed. If you think it is look into the twelfth chapter of Romans again, and see if you haven't made a grave mistake. That is, we can't hate man. The Word of God is the best teacher you have. It behooves us to study to know what our teachers have to say to us on the subject of hate, and then act accordingly. If we do that we shall find that we are making this a very good old world to live in."

THE CHALLENGE OF THE KLAN

"We must be operative Klansmen. We will not take the law into our own hands, for we are law-abiding citizens. Yet we will see to it that our great institution shall continue to make vital its spiritual purposes; achieve its laudable objects, and attain its lofty ideals. We rededicate ourselves to insure unity of organization, and guarantee an effective form of government, and pledge our voice, our loyalty, our manhood and our sacred honor to enforce the same— that justice and honor may be done the sacred memory of those who wrought through our mystic society during that early period. . . .

"Let us beware of the temptation to misrepresent for the sake of effect; let us remember that there are business and social methods which break the heart as well as ruin character; that 'a falling drop at last will cleave a stone.' Let us not allow gossip or slander to ride on rumor's tongue but rather let us 'set a watch over our mouths, and keep the door of our lips,' remembering that a tale bearer is worse than a thief, but that a golden mind stoops not to shows of dross." (From *The Kluxer*, Dayton, Ohio.)

———

"The Ku Klux Klan—America's greatest patriotic brotherhood—marches on!

"The past summer season has witnessed the greatest

144

gathering together of America's native-born Protestant, American men that this country has ever known.

"From Maine to California, and from the Great Lakes to the Gulf of Mexico, the Fiery Cross has blazed its message of patriotic redemption in every city and hamlet, and prairie and valley, in this great land of democracy and freedom—striking fear into the hearts of America's enemies and, in some places, goading them to deeds of desperation.

"In spite of malicious propaganda in the columns of an unprincipled press—in spite of misrepresentation and abuse from enemies—in spite of misunderstanding and criticism on the part of those who should be friends—THE KU KLUX KLAN IS MARCHING ON TO CERTAIN VICTORY.

"It has no desire to control the politics of our nation, but it does expect to arouse the decent citizenship of America to such an extent that those who believe in righteous government and free institutions will arouse from their slumbers of half a century and take possession of that which is rightfully their heritage.

"In other words—the Ku Klux Klan hopes to Americanize America." (From *The Patriot*, St. Louis, Missouri.)

THE CHALLENGE OF THE KLAN

KLAN NOT FOR PERSONAL GAIN

"When the writer became a member of the great
Masonic fraternity he was told: 'You will get out
of Masonry just what you put into it—no more, no
less.' It was a lesson that made a lasting impression
on us. The same thing is true of Klankraft. Neither
is an agency for self-gain or selfish ambition. Those
who take the vows of either fraternity with the intent
that they do so only for personal gain are unworthy
as Klansmen or as Masons. . . .

"The Klan is not essentially an employment bureau,
although in its exercise of Klannishness it may aid
many a worthy brother in securing employment; it is
not a means of advancing private political ambitions,
although as a guardian of their own interests, it may
wield a mighty influence in the election of good men
to office; it is not a selling agency to enhance the
commercial and industrial interests of its members,
although in guarding their business interests it will
ever be 'truly Klannish toward Klansmen in all things
honorable.'

"Ideals, great nation-wide ideals, in the reflex of
which must all men be blessed, are the goal of Klankraft. The selfish, the trivial, the petty, the elevation
of the individual above the masses, the subordination
of the general good to the sordid grasping for per-

146

sonal gain—these things we are sworn to discourage. Is our oath a sacred obligation, or is it a meaningless jumble of high-sounding phrases? Unless the heart is right, no oath ever made any man a true Mason or an honest Klansman. If he measures his membership by the question, 'What's in it for me?' he should have the manhood to get out and not foist his selfishness upon others more worthy.—A Mason and a Klansman." (From *The Arkansas Traveller,* Little Rock, Arkansas.

———————

Even the advertising in these sheets is not without considerable interest. Some books offered in these advertisements are of the kind referred to as having been put out by the Know-nothings; the most vicious kind of hate-creating propaganda possible. *The Fellowship Forum* advertises *The Suppressed Truth about the Assassination of Abraham Lincoln,* including the oath of the Knights of the Golden Circle, which the advertisement assures us, "should be in every Protestant American's library."

The Protestant Standard advertises *The Glorious Pope and the Lowly Jesus,* and also, *Romanism versus Christianity, a ringing indictment proving Catholicism unpatriotic, un-American, un-Christian.*

The Patriot offers *Convent Cruelties, A True Story, by ex-Nun Helen Jackson, Author and victim.*

THE CHALLENGE OF THE KLAN

In addition to these there is a very distinct Klannish flavor about the ordinary business advertisement. Most notable are the expressions "100 per cent" and the use of the three "K's." We have, for example, in *The Kluxer,* "The Klean Koal Klanners," a man who "Kleans Klothes Klean," a garage which promises "Krippled Kars Kured," and another speaks of the beauties of a "Klean Krank Kase." As to the "100 per cent" people they are of all kinds. Evidently some women favor this class of men for a widow advertises for lodgers, and specifies that they must be "Hundred Percenters."

It would not be fair to fail to point out that the anti-Klan propaganda fully matches that of the Klan in virulence but, since the Klan rather than its enemies is under consideration, there is no need to illustrate this.

Klan officials deny responsibility for these publications, except for *The Fiery Cross* and *The Night-Hawk,* its official organs, and a few other papers it has recently bought, which are not subject to the same criticism as the other sheets. The Klan has no control over these raging, unofficial outpourings, they declare, and some editors are not even Klansmen, but are merely seeking profit by catering to Klan feeling. This is likely true; yet the very defense is an admission of the wide-spread religious prejudice in Klan ranks, since there is profit in such screeds.

This seems to be another of the situations which

148

the present régime inherited and has not yet straightened out. Some efforts, with small success, were made last spring and summer to tone down the rabid Klan press. Now a new plan is under way; Milton Elrod, an Indianian, who of all the Klansmen I have met is most frank to admit faults and urge remedies, has been appointed to organize a string of Klan papers throughout the country which shall be under absolute control and shall reform or drive out the present sheets. He has begun his task, and from the tone of the papers already bought it is evident that when his work has been done, a very different verdict would have to be rendered on the Klan press. At present, "blatherskite" seems about the kindest adjective that can be used.

Dr. Evans summed up the Klan's official attitude toward these papers as follows:

"One of the greatest problems the Klan could possibly have is obviously the control of newspapers as well as of individuals who, without authority, attempt to speak for the movement. There are no official Klan publications except *The Imperial Night-Hawk* and *The Fiery Cross*. A great many small country weeklies, with editors who are not even Klansmen have used the hate programme and the Klan movement as a vehicle to increase circulation, generally without success. They do not deserve any.

"The Klan weeklies, which we are now founding, will speak authoritatively for the first time. The establishment of these papers has been found necessary in order to carry true vision and understanding of the organization to the American public. Klan lecturers never appear in the open, and all Klan meetings where the public is admitted are by invitation only, the non-members being brought by individual Klansmen.

"I may add that the annunciation or interpretation of Klan principles from the pulpits of churches by ministers is never authorized, and is only the expression of individual opinions, ofttimes badly informed."

The third type of propaganda is the "whispers." As with any kind of whispering propaganda it is practically impossible to prove authorship; and the Klan's secrecy makes it possible always to deny responsibility. But there are certain whispers which appear so regularly wherever Klan activity is great that they must be considered part of the campaign, either as deliberate promulgations or as a natural undertone.

Most of these are revivals of the standard mythology about the Roman church; stories that a rifle is buried under a Catholic Church or under the Knights of Columbus Hall whenever a Catholic boy is born; that the Knights of Columbus hold secret drills, that priests seduce women at confessional, and so forth. There are current accusations; that the Catholic vote is controlled by the priests and used to corrupt political officials, that Catholic and Jewish capital controls and prints seventy per cent. of the country's newspapers, that there is a Papal conspiracy to get control of

THE BUSINESS OF "KLUXING"

America as shown by the plan to move the Vatican
to America (the denial from Rome has not stopped
this story), that Catholics have more than their proportion of office holders, that there is a Catholic-
Jewish alliance aiming at control of the public schools,
which has been so successful that in New York City
no Protestant can reach high office in the schools,
and that the criticism of the Y. M. C. A. during the
war was started by the Catholics and Jews, the former
under orders from Rome. This latter whisper has
had the interesting result of greatly increasing the
prosperity of the "Y" in some places.

There are fewer whispers about the Jews, and what
there are mostly follow the charges made two or
three years ago by *The Dearborn Independent*, alleging a world-wide Jewish money conspiracy, Jewish
backing for revolutionary movements and Jewish ambitions for the control of America. The large number
of Jewish advisers around Wilson when he was president are pointed out and there are very dirty whispers
to account for the influence they had with him and
with other public men. Finally Jews, Catholics to a
lesser extent, and aliens in general, are credited with
a natural pre-eminence in crime, vice and the corruption of officials.

One particular whisper is interesting enough to re-
peat in detail. It has to do with the dollar bills of
the issue of 1917, the ones bearing a portrait of
Washington. This bill is supposed to have been cov-

151

ered with Catholic symbols as a result of a defiant and impudent scheme of Catholics in the Bureau of Printing and Engraving. On its face, according to the whisper, there are: A portrait of some Pope in the upper left corner decorations, various hailing and recognition signals of the Knights of Columbus being made by members of the group depicting the discovery of America by Columbus, and some snakes and a portrait of St. Patrick in the lower left corner decorations. On the reverse the decorations of the ornate "E's" are supposed to show the Catholic cross, and the big figure "1" is declared to represent a crozier, the decoration over it a bishop's mitre, and so forth. The whole idea is that the bill symbolizes the watchful eye which the popes have had on America from the moment of its discovery, and their intention of dominating it. The story goes on that when President Harding discovered the profanation he discharged the head of the bureau.

This is most effective propaganda. The bill actually is a curious one; it takes no great imagination to see several of the things alleged. It is even true that the bureau head was discharged, though it was for getting the serial numbers on liberty bonds mixed up. The real weakness of the story is that the plates from which the bill is printed were first made as long ago as 1868 and have been used off and on ever since! But hundreds of thousands believe the story utterly and every good Klansman, when he gets one of these

bills, tears off the corner with the "pope's picture."
It is amazing that so silly a performance—supposing
it to be true—could cause such furor, yet thousands
take it as proof that Catholics are disloyal, flout the
power of the United States and expect the Pope to
rule America!

Before dropping these phases of kluxing, it should
be noted that the counter-propaganda is every bit as
bad as that of the Klan in its worst phases. Not only
publications but the whispers, the covert and unproved
charges, the defamation—all are unspeakable. The
counter-prejudice even goes so far that a very solemn
New York paper, after many well-justified attacks
on Klan violence, came out recently with an editorial
in justification of the mobbing of a Klan delegation
because it tried to put a wreath on a soldiers' monu-
ment! Yet it was the Klan itself that called out all
these devils of prejudice, and it must bear much of
the blame when they turn on it.

Two more things about Klan propaganda. First,
it is highly adaptable. It makes use of resentment
against alien farmers in Ohio, against Sabbath violation in Indiana, bootlegging in Kansas, alien labor in
the factories, Catholic office-holders where there are
any—and also where there are not!—a Jew's defense
of unrestricted immigration, high taxes, high railroad
rates, grafting contractors, parochial schools, the lat-
est local scandal—use of any and every resentment
that is handy. The Kleagles everywhere get inside

the community psychology and use it with great skill.

The second point is the great value to the Klan of opposition, especially when it is illegal and violent. Every case of anti-Klan persecution, and there are many, is used to prove the perversion of Americanism and the domination of officials by Catholics, Jews, or aliens. The fact that a boy was fined $100 for selling a copy of *The Fiery Cross* was one of the best talking points in the campaign that gave the Klan a half million members in Indiana. The attacks on Klan parades in several places brought swarms of recruits. "If we could have a riot a week, we'd own the country in a year," one Klan organizer told me, and he gave figures to prove it. Almost all Klansmen firmly believe that these attacks were ordered by Catholic priests, a sort of religious persecution, and were also ordered stopped because they failed to check the Klan.

Curiously, this has had a reaction somewhat favorable to the Catholics, for, as one Klan official said: "If they're fools enough to do a thing like that, they can't really be very dangerous." I assured him that I didn't believe the Church was responsible, but do not know yet whether my remark hurt or helped the Klan—assuming that I convinced him.

Thus the evidence seems conclusive that the business of kluxing carries with it not only stimulation of patriotism and of a sense of civic duty, but very grave evils. These include the appeal to and stimula-

154

tion of hatred and prejudice, the circulation of stories some of which are untrue and all of which are circulated to increase class solidarity and national division, and the gathering of all kinds of riff-raff who can not possibly sympathize with the high aims the Klan professes. The Klan claims that it regenerates and uses such men. Even so, many evils remain; evils which it is nothing less than criminal to foster if the Klan is run for either profit or personal power, as so many believe.

Even if the Klan's own statement of its purpose be accepted, it is still possible to condone these evils on only one ground; that its purposes are high enough, its chances of achieving them good enough and the incidental reforms it makes important enough, to offset the damage it does. This plea has to be made for many organized movements and the Klan is certainly entitled to whatever benefit it may give. It can also plead in defense the efforts it is making to suppress these evils, and if it should succeed in stamping them out, as it has practically stamped out violence, its position would be immensely strengthened.

But there would always remain all the disruptive force implied in its programme of "native, white, Protestant supremacy."

CHAPTER VII

THE LURE OF THE WHITE MASK

SOME measure of the value of the Ku Klux idea to members of the Klan can be found in the price they pay to join. The amount is not large—$10.00 for initiation and $5.00 for regalia—yet as the price of getting behind an idea that is considerable. One can join a good many movements for less, and among the people who make up the bulk of the Klan strength even $15.00 is not treated with disrespect. Any one who has ever tried to enlist people, at a price, in any general movement will testify that it is no mean achievement to induce four million men to pay anything at all.

To this cash cost must be added the fact that most members have joined the Klan in the face of strong public disapproval and often of actual persecution. Add, too, the attitude of members toward the Klan, the serious view they take of its doctrine, their often almost fanatical devotion, and it begins to be plain that the Klan means something rather important to them. It may not be what the Klan stands for officially, it may be something warped or even vicious, but the Klan seems to them to offer something they want badly, something they are willing to pay for both in cash and in service.

When there are four million people held in this way by an idea there can be no doubt that the idea has power. Imperial Wizard Evans declares that it is the most potent idea in America and there is much truth in this. But he means the Klan idea as he sees it, and it must be remembered that the real driving force is not his idea, but the thought in the minds of the Klansmen themselves, often something very different.

Perhaps the first thing to do in attempting to get at the spirit which animates and unites these four millions, is to set to one side the excrescences, for they are both noisy and numerous and easily mistaken for the real embodiment of the Klan.

As soon as any organization begins to gain power certain kinds of men join it for personal profit. There will be promoters and organizers, second-rate politicians, business men looking for trade, sharks seeking prey, criminals hoping for protection and chronic failures who will try anything. The more powerful the organization, the more numerous and active will be these parasites, hypocrites and grafters. The Klan has its full share of them, and they are often prominent, since high places are the best for the grinding of private axes. But after all they are parasites and

157

do not represent the idea and spirit that gave the Klan its great growth. They are important in many ways, for they have influence, but one can not measure the real Klan by them.

Most numerous of these are the cheap politicians who hope to push themselves by means of the Klan's strength. There are several varieties, men who are about to be defeated for re-election, men who have never been able to get far in political preferment, men who are involved in all the piddling graft that goes with local administration, and other kinds who work in the same way. They usually try to build up a personal following among the Klansmen, and are always a source of irritation to the higher officers who are constantly struggling against them.

The next most numerous class is the business getter. The principles of the Klan encourage trading among Klansmen wherever possible. It is inevitable that a considerable number of men should see in this a quick road to wealth. Especially where a Klan has been newly organized, signs of this activity appear on every side. There will be crosses over the doors of shops, the triple K monogram on the doors or windows, the use of "100%" in all kinds of advertising. This also the Klan officials are trying to stop, and orders have been issued recently forbidding the use in business of these or any other symbols of the Klan.

Undoubtedly a goodly number of the Kleagles and Klan propagandists in general are in the business for revenue only. Another kind of parasite who appears in considerable numbers is the petty criminal who hopes to get protection from the Klan. There is one southwestern state where the head of the Klan is alleged to be the state's boss bootlegger, and there are many places in which there is talk of this kind of law-breaking in connection with the Klan. Some similar situations have to my knowledge been cleared up from inside; there are others in which the higher officials are now trying to get evidence. They seem wholly sincere in their efforts to disinfect, but the job is far from being done.

Coming to the real Klan spirit, there are such differences between the Klan as it appears in Georgia and Texas, in Ohio and New York, that there is room for doubt whether it actually is moved by a single thought. Yet I believe that it is; that there is a unifying idea, a certain least common denominator of purpose, which may be found and defined. There is, of course, the "native, white, Protestant supremacy" of the Klan creed, but that seems to be a formula of action and a theory of social organization rather than an end or purpose in itself, and it is not by any means always involved in Klan activities. The true spirit seems to be something deeper, and at bottom far healthier, although it sometimes shows in dangerous and even abominable forms.

This fundamental and unifying idea is nothing more abnormal than a passion for reform, as Dr. Evans has said. Yet it is abnormal, too, for with the Klan this very common trait has an intensity, a directness and a concept of personal duty to do something, such as are seldom found. And it produces very unusual manifestations. This is partly because the Klan reaches certain classes seldom stirred by such sentiments and therefore unfamiliar with the accepted procedure; people of simple, direct and intense emotions who act accordingly. Partly, too, it is due to the violent prejudices and instincts the Klan doctrine arouses. But whether the immediate aim be the regulation of a neighbor's conduct, or the ousting of parochial schools or of corrupt officials, reform of some sort has been the moving spirit of the Klan wherever I have seen it.

This is not a blanket approval—far from it. There can be little debate that the reform spirit on the whole is useful, but only when kept within limits. The line is not well defined; sincere people who agree in disapproving drink, tobacco, dancing, betting and the like are to be found on both sides of the question of how far one's own virtues should regulate other people's vices. But there is always a saving popular resistance which prevents most reforms from going too far. The Klan aims to go very far indeed; even officially it attacks questions and employs methods to which we are not hardened, in its programme it applies race and religion standards we are in the habit of ignoring, and its individual members have aims and use methods considerably further from normal than the leaders wish.

Moreover, reform at its best has some unlovely aspects. It always implies a "holier than thou" attitude, it always makes trouble and disturbs the even tenor of life, it is often so beneficial to the reformers that their motives may easily be questioned, and it sometimes shows a narrow, meddling, officious, unjust and even cruel spirit. Often, too, the pleasure of reforming other people appeals more strongly than does the good to be done. These things appear prominently in some members of the Klan; indeed it often seems that the Klan is demonstrating just how bad reform may be. It is no wonder the opposition is violent. But, however distorted, the Klan idea is at bottom nothing more or less than a new and violent outbreak of our good old American habit of re-arranging the world. There is much expert testimony to the effect that we do this oftener and worse than any other people on earth.

When all allowances are made for other motives—love of excitement, self-interest and brutality—this reform idea is still to be seen even in the worst of the Klan actions, the night-riding and maltreatment of neighbors. This particular phase is worth study, since if one can understand it, then it will be easier to understand also many of the less vicious but still dangerous practises of Klansmen.

There is no need to list the evils of night-riding,

but it is always worth while to find why comparatively decent people take to doing utterly wrong things. I put this question to the governor of a state which has been peculiarly cursed with this noxious crime—a man who has done much to stop violence and has been especially active against Klan mobs. The conditions he describes are still to be found in many places, both in the South and elsewhere.

"You understand that I don't defend mob action in any case or form," the governor began. "Yet there is something to be said for it—sometimes. There have been cases where I had to admit some sympathy. But I'm afraid this can hardly be understood by you people who live in communities so well protected that police corruption means at worst bootlegging and poker games, and a 'crime wave' means that there is about one chance in fifty thousand that you will suffer from something worse than sneak-thievery.

"Try to imagine, if you can, what it would mean to live where it is practically impossible to enforce any law, where intimidation and abuse are customary, theft common, arson not unusual, and murder occasional—all unpunishable. There are such places. Sparse settlements, family feuds, powerful criminal elements, make it almost impossible to get sure law enforcement in these plague spots. And you can't reform them by the ballot, for the toughs control the elections. If any man takes the lead in trying to clean up, he will suffer. If he is not killed, his barns will be burned, his crops ruined, his stock destroyed or stolen, his women folks insulted.

"There is another type of case in which we also find legal action either impossible or unsatisfactory. This has to do with the reputation of decent women. Every one knows that it is entirely possible for a good woman to become involved in trouble without any fault of her own, but in such circumstances that if the facts became known it would do her irreparable injury. Even when injury would not result, for her to appear on the stand and testify would be an ordeal unspeakable. We, in the South, and this is especially true in the country districts, will go to almost any length to save women from these things. There is one case of night-riding now before the courts in this State which, I believe, will never be prosecuted for this reason. The injustice that would be done a certain woman if the whole story were told is far greater than any advantage that would come from convicting the culprits.

"So there has always been a tendency in this state —and some others—to form vigilance committees to handle such situations. You can call it cowardice if you want to, but when unknown men apply pressure to the tough element, they can get results and still be safe from reprisals. Scores of places have been cleaned up in just that way. And when people are suffering you can't expect them to worry about the danger that the same methods will be unjustly used some other time.

"That was the condition which gave the Klan its first start in this state. The best people didn't join, of course, and a lot of the uneducated, poor white trash did. Lately the Klan has changed its methods and some of the better class are joining. But they'll lose out if they can't keep on cleaning up."

This testimony would be enough even if standing alone. But the condition seems to have been general in all the states where much night-riding occurred. The story of what happened in Tulsa is lurid and extreme, but typical of conditions in many towns.

Two years ago Tulsa was under almost absolute control of the criminals whose influence in politics outweighed that of any decent element.

Bootlegging, dope peddling and vice flourished openly. Highway robbery, which the Southwest calls "hi-jacking," was common, and on one celebrated evening a gang took possession of one of the main roads outside of the city and for hours systematically looted all traffic. Murder was frequent, few decent men and no decent woman left shelter at night. Officers seldom interfered, those who did were shot down with impunity, and in the few cases where criminals were convicted, they were usually promptly pardoned.

As has been the case so often in this country, the citizens finally took to illegal means to restore order. The reformers became night-riders. The methods used were direct, brutal and effective. Around Tulsa they armed themselves, went out in automobiles as bait for the "hi-jackers" and when they were held up, shot to kill. Some of them were killed too, but within a few weeks such "hi-jackers" as were left alive moved to other fields. With bootleggers, dope peddlers, and so on, less drastic means were used. Men who were suspected—sometimes women—were given rump trials and soundly whipped—the kind of raw-hiding from which it takes the strongest man weeks to recover. With the gangs thus broken a reform ticket was elected and peace returned to the community.

There is no question that the Klan played a large part in this. Governor Walton's courts assembled a great deal of evidence, some of which was apparently perjured, but succeeded actually in convicting only four Klansmen—one case out of more than sixty. Klansmen themselves, however, have admitted complicity in a great many other cases, and have defended their actions on the ground that this was the only possible way to bring about reform. Even in the Mer Rouge horrors—whatever the facts there may be —the Klan action was taken to stop alleged criminal traffic. Thus the motive is always reform; the purpose almost always a decent one.

The governor quoted above, however, did not get at the whole reason for the appeal which night-riding makes to this particular element. It has certain attractions besides reform for simple and direct minds.

THE CHALLENGE OF THE KLAN

When Dr. Evans started his campaign which has so largely stopped violence as a Klan method, a friend in the South wrote me:

"I shall be surprised if the Southern faction agrees with Evans in the matter of violence. Those methods are the great attraction, the basis of confidence, a manner of executing justice that renders the greatest personal satisfaction."

That "personal satisfaction"—in executing justice, be it noted!—was undoubtedly one of the lures of the white masks, until a few months ago. And my friend's estimate was correct, too, for the Evans campaign was followed by a falling off of Klan strength in the night-riding states. There are signs now that a new and better element is joining the Klan in these states, but there is no doubt that the methods used, as well as the reforms to be made, helped give the Klan its hold.

There is another motive, almost as indefensible as the urge to mob violence, but easier to sympathize with and far more wide-spread, which has brought many members into the Klan and is still bringing them. This is the desire to correct evils—often personal ones—which are out of reach of the law, through mass action of various kinds. Most of us bear these ills, especially those of other people, with such grins, shrugs or curses as our natures call for, but great numbers see in the Klan an opportunity for reform along just these lines.

THE LURE OF THE WHITE MASK

"I wish I was as simple minded as some folks," one circuit judge confided. "Then I'd join the Klan. One of the things that make a judge's life hard is the wrongs for which there is no legal remedy; the unfair but not criminal methods of slick crooks, the betrayals of women where more harm than good is done if the law is called in, the oppressions of money-lenders, the laziness of men who let their children starve—all so common we take them for granted, and nice folks think they're melodramatic, but all devilish, just the same. I can't do anything about them.

"I can't stand, either, for action against them that isn't based on trial and evidence. But the Klan doesn't worry about that. They are all neighbors and believe they know what's happened and they let it go at that. They want action, and they think that's what they're there for and go at it bald headed. Usually they're right, so far as substantial justice is concerned. I don't blame them—much."

Many Klansmen avow this motive freely enough.

"I joined just to see that they got after ——" one friend told me, naming a notorious cheat.

"I hear the Klan kind of fixes up things that ain't right," another said. "Well, So-and-so has fixed it up with the store so I can't get good materials, and my work's so bad I can't make a living. I'm going to join and see if it can't be stopped." And join he did.

"My sister's husband is off raising hell in Indiana

and don't send her enough to live on," remarked the third. "They've passed word to the Klan out there."

These are only a few. The Grand Dragon of one state told me he got twenty requests a week for action in just such cases; another put his calls at fifty. I believe that on the whole the desire for this kind of reform has been more powerful than any other one thing in drawing men into the Klan. It is a very human and often "neighborly" desire, supported by the simpler morality, and it is difficult for "plain-minded" folks to see the gross violation of fundamental principles, which makes it vicious. I even notice that people who do see this evil and disapprove on principle, find it hard to work up much indignation over actual cases where they believe the victims are guilty. Action along these lines is not on the official Klan programme, and is being discouraged by the leaders, but without either the vigor or the success of the campaign against violence.

These two are the great unavowed motives in the Klan. Other motives, still reformatory, follow closely the lines of the propaganda.

"They're going to give Ohio and Indiana the biggest cleaning up you ever heard of," a Veterans' Bureau Worker reports. "They're after every little thing—crooked officials, crooked business, vice, crime, Sabbath breaking, poor schools, and the rest."

This is the official Klan programme, it will be seen. Even in the "night-riding states" I found many who had joined for these reasons. And everywhere, of course, there are very large numbers who have joined because the Klan seems to them to offer a solution to the great national questions of hyphenism and unassimilated immigration.

One of the strongest motives in drawing men into the Klan, or perhaps it would be more correct to say that one of the strongest desires now in the minds of Klansmen, is for reform of the public schools. This is already so important and is growing so rapidly that it may very soon become the dominant issue in the Klan programme.

There are several reasons for dissatisfaction with the public schools to-day in many parts of the country. The simplest, of course, is that they do not equip their pupils for either successful or comfortable living, or for good citizenship. Klansmen believe that the schools to-day very deliberately fail to teach the essentials of government, of religion, of morals, or of patriotism. They believe that there is a set purpose behind this, and that the schools have been intentionally and traitorously debauched.

They blame the Catholics. They declare that it is the Catholics who have backed laws preventing the teaching of the Bible in the schools, who have opposed the making of adequate appropriations for the public schools in order to save money for the priest-controlled parochial schools, and who also encourage members of the Roman church to become teachers and then to teach as poorly as possible. The Klan believes that the Catholics hope eventually by these means not only to destroy the public schools, but so to lower the intelligence of the nation that it will be an easy prey.

There are an immense number of men and women in the Klan who have either joined for the purpose of affecting education, or who have now made it their chief interest.

This, then, is the nucleus of thought around which the Klan has been built—reform, sometimes selfish and sometimes public-spirited, sometimes lawless, sometimes merely meddlesome, sometimes well-founded and using the entirely proper methods of opinion and votes. Often it is a mixture of all these elements. The means used are determined by the state of civilization of the men or the communities in which the Klan has called this thought into action.

But always it is reform of one kind or another, and however warped or misdirected, it is almost always aimed at some real wrong or abuse. It may err in ascribing the evils to Catholics, Jews, or aliens, but the evils themselves are actual enough.

In other words the Klan movement seems to be another expression of the general unrest and dissatisfaction with both local and national conditions—the high cost of living, social injustice and inequality, mal-administration of justice, political corruption, hyphenism, disunity, unassimilated and conflicting

170

ideals and standards—which are distressing all thoughtful men. The Klan is strong because it offers what no one else has offered: a solution which, whether right or not, is fundamental and all-embracing in that it calls for a return to a time-honored standard. The Klan, also, has been wise enough not to promise any complete cure.

This is the nucleus, but it is not all the Klan. There must be added the accretions which gather to any growing organization and a few which are peculiar to the Klan itself. Among the latter are the "haters" whose prejudices are always strong and who react violently to the Klan propaganda; the hot-heads who are attracted by the chance for mysterious and violent action; the youths who want "fun, romance and swagger," and the cowards who hope under cover to satisfy private grudges. Among the normal burrs are the "joiners," the people who go with the crowd, those who have definite ends that may be helped by the support of any organization, and the parasites.

This study of Klan psychology would be incomplete without a word on "nigger-haters." The Klan of the 'sixties was directed against the Negro, and undoubtedly this particular prejudice was large in the men who formed the new Klan. But I can only report that I have not found the Negro question as a motive anywhere in the Klan. I suppose that it exists, but in my entire inquiry and in many long discussions with both Klansmen and Klan enemies, the Negro has never been mentioned until I myself brought him up.

The attitude of Dr. Evans toward these various motives in Klansmen has been rather fully reported in previous chapters. Two further remarks of his bear on the subject. I had pointed out the large number who joined from motives very different from those the Klan avows.

"Human emotions and human motives are the same the world over and since the world began," he replied. "Of course, in a vast organization, with millions of members, there are bound to be undesirable individuals. This is true in the most serious way during the propagating period. There is an intangible something, however, in the Klan that searches out the hearts of men, and it has been the experience that the man who has joined for selfish or intolerant reasons is very quickly converted or driven out."

"Is not a large part of the membership of the unbalanced, hot-headed type of young men?" was another question.

"No, I would not say that," he replied. "I would say that the Klan is composed of young, rather than old men, but it is the young men of the balanced minds who are the stamina of the nation. I have seen audiences of many kinds, and I will say that Klan audiences will compare very favorably with any audience you have ever seen."

It is impossible to make more than a guess at the

proportion of the various motives which lead men to join the Klan. It differs in every community. But taking the country as a whole I should guess that the parasites number less than five per cent. of the whole, the actual haters and trouble-hunters another five per cent. and the "joiners" about twenty per cent. The remaining seventy per cent. seem sincere reformers, however mistaken. About half of this seventy per cent., I believe, is moved largely by the desire to remedy things which can not be reached by law—the largest single element—and most of the rest by hope of local reform of some rather valuable kind. Those primarily moved to join by the national aims of the Klan I should not put above ten per cent. But all these motives overlap, though I should also guess that at least seventy per cent. of the Klansmen would work with some vigor for local reforms, and almost as many would support the national programme.

There is one more thing about the composite mind of the Klan which may be interpreted in different ways, but can not be ignored. This is a certain intensity, purposefulness, sometimes unselfishness, which the Klan seems to instil into the majority of its members. There is of course a great background for emotionalism in the Klan's aims and forms of appeal; the Klan seizes on this, strengthens and uses it. To many Klansmen the Klan doctrines have come with the force of revelation, sacred, over-mastering, and with most of the elements of religious conversion.

THE CHALLENGE OF THE KLAN

This is actually a spiritual force like the rather narrow but very intense and often devoted emotional conviction, which has been the chief driving power in the more evangelistic of the Protestant denominations. Every Klansman I have met, save one, is a Fundamentalist, and it is easy to understand why an organization such as the Klan, full of ritualism and symbolism and demanding much blind faith, should naturally be Fundamental.

I asked one of my friends in the Klan, who has had very wide opportunities for observation, to define for me the spiritual side of Ku Kluxism. He wrote as follows:

"If I were to try in my feeble way to classify the spiritual vision of the Klan, I would merely say that the thoughts which are behind the political idea that good Republicans and good Democrats can, as Klansmen, maintain and perpetuate a government free from present party bias, make Klansmen believe also that the Klan can hold to the ideas of John Calvin and yet correct within the Protestant church those evils that seem to be inimical to the best interests of the church.

"They feel that its old system of 'authority' needs revamping. They would not tamper with the fundamental creed, but I have heard many a good Protestant Klansman—preachers, if you please—point out that we should not too bitterly criticize the Roman Catholic church, if at all, so long as certain 'despotisms' and

174

'authoritative conditions' remain in the Protestant churches.

"I believe the keynote of the Klansmen spiritually is, that they should hold rigidly to the fundamental idea of Protestanism, that they would not change the 'faith' and the 'semblance of symbolism,' but *would* change in a manner 'the machinery of government of the church itself.'" For instance, fifty-two per cent. of a certain Methodist Assembly found itself face to face with a bishop and a board that were opposed to the Klan, modernists, in their sympathies at least. These men of the fifty-two per cent. stood fast, were denied their salary increases, and some of them were given most inferior appointments. But some of them, with their *Klan congregations solidly behind them, dared the Bishop to make a single move;* and he certainly did not!

"Whether or not the Klan means rebellion in the Protestant church is something that will require very careful and deep investigation, but it certainly bears many signs pointing in that direction.

"I believe the Klan would do the same thing to Protestantism that it hopes to do to the American Government, and it seems to be entirely free from any thought of denominationalism. It certainly is free from the intolerance of one denomination toward another. It is significant that Klansmen do attend church, and that the Klan has had a remarkable influence in the increase of church attendance. They go in large groups from first one church to another, and one of the secrets of the organization is the vast financial aid rendered by the Klan to worthy churches and needy pastors.

"I would make just a fair guess that more than two million dollars were contributed to churches last year by Klansmen, without any strings whatsoever, merely with the idea of giving support to fundamental Protestantism.

"The spiritual inspiration of the Klan is its deepest quality, far deeper, I believe, than the things you have been discussing in your writings, but, like other parts of the Klan, and its symbolism, carefully guarded, silent but mighty and potential. There is running through the Klan a spirit of vast humility. Its members believe that the danger to Protestantism lies in Catholic encroachments, and that Protestants (free from creeds and denominationalism) must stoutly resist or be driven from the field. They believe that Protestantism as a religion must be made as militant as the Klan is in its political activities, and that it should appeal to all men who are teachable and aspiring, who measure themselves by ideals of loyalty. They feel the Klan is the power by which they, Klansmen, can do their best work for America and Protestantism itself.

"Klansmen insist on personal character of a high type because they believe that the value of the service they can render in the spiritual field naturally depends on the quality of the men who serve. They certainly believe in the composite Protestant mind. It stands in the life of the Klansman for spiritual deeds and their exemplification in every-day life, civic, political and religious, all straight Protestant Americanism and, if you please, Calvinism.

"I do not agree with all these points, but am trying to give you in a brief way what I know of the composite mind of the Klan on this subject. I believe that it stands for a 'religion of spirit' and would get rid of a lot of 'religion of authority.' It would draw the line further and more completely between the idea of authority expressed in the Roman Catholic church and in its own. But it does not want to give up for one minute the idea of 'faith as a deposit.' It does not want to disbelieve, but wishes to continue to accept as true all the miracle stories in the Bible, that are 'not unworthy of God the Father and Our Lord Jesus Christ.' It does not wish any 'scientific tests' or proof, in these things.

"So, there you have it, the best that I can give you, an apparent contradiction, an enigma if there ever was one. The Klan can stand on the Protestant faith. It certainly is wiping out denominationalism and it is certainly bringing men back to a more rigid adherence to the fundamental idea of Protestantism.

"I believe the element of symbolism can be applied to the spiritual side of the organization fully and unreservedly, and that the Klan affords Protestants an opportunity to get together on a common ground, to consider the Master as a Patriot for the great cause, and to work for the idea that *the kingdom of God on earth, the rule of righteousness in the personal life and social relationship of the Klansmen, should be to all mankind identical with the cause of Jesus Christ.* The Klansman will adhere to his Methodist affiliations, his Christian, United Brethren, or other denomination, in about the same way a Klansman adheres to such fraternal affiliations, as the Knights of Pythias, Odd Fellows, etc. He will accept the Klan as a common cause, and in the Klan he becomes not only a Christian but a Patriot for the cause of the Klan, which he firmly believes to be the Cause of the Master. I believe that you can rely upon a Klansman at all times to be loyal to the Cause.

"Undoubtedly these men are looking to the Klan to point out the common ground, and I believe the most potent thing in the Klan itself, from a religious point of view, is that it will solidify a straight Protestant faith against the common enemy and for the common good.

"You have made the point that the Klan is a protest movement, and what is a Protestant but a protest-ant? Each has thought his particular denomination the best form of expression of 'protest' and probably his particular form of religious symbolism; but he sees in the Klan a more definite, more militant, more operative 'protestantism.'

THE LURE OF THE WHITE MASK

"The Twelfth Chapter of Romans, which is a part of the Klan ritual, the fourth, fifth, and sixth verses, certainly cover the point:

" 'For as we have many members in one body, and all members have not the same *office;*
" 'So we, being many, are one body in Christ, and every one members one of *another.*
" 'Having then gifts differing according to the grace that is given to us, whether prophecy, let us prophesy according to the proportion of faith.' "

The effect produced by this kind of fervid conviction naturally depends on the character of the individual man, but it is to be felt in some form in every contact with the Klan. It rises sometimes to the pitch of fierce fanaticism, with all the shocking and terrible splendor of that form of obsession. Nothing less, for example, could have held the paraders standing in the streets of Carnegie while brick-bats and bullets felled a quarter of their number. This was the martyr spirit. But this same intensity may also produce a narrow, intolerant, irascible attitude, impatient of opposition or question, which classes all outsiders as enemies and strikes with equal vigor at crimes, corruption or criticism. A correspondent in Dallas who is fighting the Klan bitterly, writes on this phase:
"I have reason to believe I know the psychology of the Klansmen. It is a modern Mohammedanism more than anything else. And great is the Grand Titan.

It is semi-religious, yet it is a religion of violence, propagated by violence, and its adherents are modern fuzzy-wuzzies in business clothes. No more cowards than other men, but selfish, egotistic and dangerous modern fanatics, and at the slightest show of disagreement the sword is brought into play and the 'Christian dog' is slain. (Except that the sword is the six-gun.)"

There is truth in this condemnation, yet it would fit Cromwell's Ironsides or the Salem Puritans—any strongly convinced body of men! The Klan spirit does not express itself with six-guns in Ohio and Indiana, where the Klan strength is now centered, but that seems a difference due chiefly to the customs of the country. The spirit is nearly as intense there even if less raw, and it can better be called devotion or consecration than fanaticism. Certainly that is the pitch at which the Klan leaders try to hold it.

But the difference is one of degree; there is still the semi-religious feeling, the resentment toward opposition, the narrowness and often intolerance. It is more than a coincidence that everywhere the Klan is linked with and supported by the narrower, less liberal churches, and that most of its members are "Fundamentalists." In Ohio, for example, all the Protestant churches are more or less involved except the Congregationalists and Unitarians.

This strong religious element in the Klan naturally leaves it wide open to attack, because of its bar against the race from which Jesus came. Probably the most effective campaigner against the Klan at present is former Governor Jim Ferguson of Texas. He is certainly no saint, and several different kinds of incongruity are involved when he attacks the Klan on religious grounds. "Big Jim's" most telling attack is the following story:

"I dreamed the other night that I had been inveigled into going outside the Klavern or whatever it is they call this here place where men go to wear bedsheets and pillow cases. While I was waiting, there came up to the door a tall man with fair hair that came down over his shoulders, and a yellow beard, and long trailing garments, and he was barefooted. And he went up and knocked on the door. Pretty soon the Klackter or Klickter or Klexter, or whatever it is they call him, came out and asked this man what he wanted. The man said he wanted to join the Klan.

" 'Are you an American?' asked this Klexter.

" 'No,' said the man with the beard, 'I do not belong to any nation.'

" 'Huh!' said the noble Knight. 'Where were you born?'

" 'I was born in Judea,' said the man.

" 'Well get the hell out of here,' said the Klexter. 'We ain't got no use for no one but native white Protestants.' "

Of course this is not a fair attack on the Klan, since Christ could not be admitted under the rules of many worthy organizations, nor become president of the United States! It is, however, an extremely effective piece of propaganda, and one tremendously painful to the religious minded Klansman.

This then, is the mind of the Klan as nearly as it can be seen. A mind with mixed motives, generally well-intentioned, confused, warped and illogical, or sane and clear in different individuals. It includes purposes very different from those the leaders profess as well as those they do avow, and prejudices and hatreds they are trying to control. And the whole is driven by an intense emotionalism which makes it a tremendous power, and doubly a menace wherever it goes wrong.

CHAPTER VIII

THE STRENGTH OF INVISIBILITY

THERE has seldom been an organization so amazingly well designed for getting what it wants as is the Ku Klux Klan. One has to go back to the unproved stories of the secret and deadly workings of the lay branch of the Society of Jesus three hundred years ago for a parallel. For the Klan is able not only to make its will effective—startlingly effective considering its numbers—but to do so with almost complete immunity and to leave those whom it attacks beating the air, helpless to strike back.

This is not accidental; the Klan has been planned and built for just this end.

It is the offspring of extremely able brains, probably those of General Forrest and his associates in the 'sixties with improvements added by experience. It is devised to permit a minority—even a minute minority—to multiply its power, to strike swiftly and silently, and to remain secure. So long as its oaths hold and its members are steadfast it can do this almost flawlessly.

183

THE CHALLENGE OF THE KLAN

Every least thing about the Klan is made to contribute to this. Just as its spirit is one of reform and its basic idea is native, white, Protestant supremacy, so its purpose focuses on direct, militant, immediate action to put its spirit and its ideas into effect all along the line. It gathers together for this all the various elements of strength which have been described in previous chapters—its secrecy, its appeal to instinct or prejudice, its careful organization, and finally its intense emotionalism—and drives them into effective action. How successful this action is will be told in the next chapter; the purpose of the present one is to study the elements of power in action, which make such success possible.

The first of these elements is the militant and military organization, with its autocratic control. This centers in the Imperial Wizard the power to order action without waste of time or confusing counsels, and it permits that sudden concentrated use of all available strength which is only possible to despotism. That in fact is the avowed object of this form of organization. Says Paul S. Etherbridge, the Imperial Klonsel:

"The form and character of our government is, however, both in theory and in practise, military, and in a sense autocratic. We ourselves have made it so.

"Article 1, Section 2, of the Constitution is very explicit on this point. Our Imperial Wizard is Commander-in-chief, and he is supreme within certain restrictions of the Constitution, and his decisions, decrees, edicts, mandates, rulings and instructions are of full authority and must be unquestionably recognized and respected by each and every citizen of the Invisible Empire.

"The military feature runs all through our plan of operation, and the autocratic form of government lies in the fact of the authority and power vested in our Imperial Wizard, and also in the method of his election. See in this connection Article 9, Section 1; where provision is made for the election of the Wizard by the Grand Dragons. Some slight criticism of this article has once or twice been suggested on the ground that the Imperial Wizard—Supreme Chief Executive of the Order—under the provisions of the said article is elected by the Grand Dragons, who are themselves subjects of his own appointment, and it has been pointed out that a similarity of operation exists in this respect between the Knights of the Ku Klux Klan and the Roman Hierarchy. It is an admitted fact that there is indeed a strong similarity between the two. In answer to the criticism arising on this account let it be remembered that no form of government in all history has developed such proficiency in handling the masses as has the Church of Rome, and we must admit that any organization, religious or otherwise, which can take a hopeless minority and with it control an overwhelming majority in a Protestant, democratic nation, like America, can not be ignored with safety.

185

THE CHALLENGE OF THE KLAN

And if the method and form of government can be
so organized as to develop to such a degree of efficiency
for the accomplishment of purposes destructive and
inimical to the free institutions of our government, is
there any good reason why the same or similar operating plans should not be perfected for the accomplishment of good, and why the same should not be made
to operate along constructive lines with the same degree of effectiveness?

"Some of the most iniquitous devices of the devil
himself are operated upon plans that develop the highest efficiency and the greatest degree of effectiveness,
but this does not mean that the devil owns the plans.
If the living Christ, a Klansman's criterion of character, could commend to his disciples methods employed by his arch enemy, why should not we, in good
faith, adopt the methods which have proved their
efficacy through twenty centuries of history, although
we denounce the ends and purposes to which they have
been diverted.

"There is another reason why our government must
be military in character. Our organization is more
than a secret order; it is a movement; in a sense,
it is a crusade. Military discipline must be maintained in our organization because we, unlike purely
civic bodies, or civic governments, are sailing un-
charted seas, and there is no precedent by which we
may be guided. Many other organizations having
somewhat similar objects and purposes, but without

the military feature, have fallen by the wayside and been forgotten. Because there is no precedent by which we can be guided, it becomes essential that one general direct the march, and that direction be accomplished only through a rigid military programme. If the time shall come when the purposes for which the Klan was organized have all been accomplished, then its members need no longer be a militant, fighting organization, and they may possibly revert into an organization something like the Veterans of Foreign Wars, or the veterans of any other crusade; but until such time, and until the purposes for which the Klan was organized have been accomplished, the military feature of the Klan must be maintained."

This rigid, concentrated power in the first place, is backed up by rigorous control over the individual members, a discipline which is well-nigh military in most ways. The words of the oath are clear: "I . . . will render at all times loyal respect and steadfast support to the Imperial authority, and will heartily heed all official mandates, decrees, edicts, rulings and instructions," and so forth. There is no limitation in this and I find none in the Constitution, yet there are some things the Wizard could not order without breaking his own oath, and there is much evidence that the leaders would be afraid to attempt authority beyond certain points. For all ordinary purposes within the aims of the Klan, however, the authority is complete.

The proof of this, in its widest manifestation, is

the sudden ceasing of night-riding throughout the whole Klan when Dr. Evans got control and issued his reform orders. But there have been even clearer evidences of the drastic control in local situations, as where Klansmen have submitted to violence without retaliation. A state-wide demonstration was given in Oklahoma when Governor Walton's gunmen made really outrageous attempts to goad the Klansmen into some kind of violence that would have justified Walton's charges and have given him an excuse for military action.

A typical performance was that at the town of Comanche, where the Klan had called one of those big open air meetings so loved by farmers. There were to be speeches, bands, an initiation and a big picnic dinner furnished by women of the churches. Some ten thousand people had gathered when twenty-five of Walton's men appeared. They had no warrants, no official right to act even if their action had been legal, as it was not. They ordered the gathering to disperse, waved weapons, threatened the men, hustled the women, kicked over the baskets of fried chicken and apple pie, and in general behaved as offensively as possible. There were enough fighting men in the crowd to have routed them easily—Oklahoma has a good many half-reformed cowboys—and the Klan officials sweat blood before they finally got the crowd broken up in peace. The fact that during the whole Walton fight, with its many irritating contacts, no single instance of Klan violence occurred, speaks volumes for the way Klansmen "heartily heed" their orders.

The third advantage derived from the military organization is the ability of the Klan to reach all the members on very short notice, and to get them into action with bewildering swiftness.

This system works amazingly well, far better than an emergency call to a militia regiment, for example. There was a case in an Ohio city where the authorities —illegally—had forbidden any Klan meeting inside the county. At five o'clock one day a national Klan speaker arrived, word of a meeting began to be circulated about six, and at eight some fifteen thousand men had gathered in a field twenty miles away, across the county line, though every one must have had to change his plans for the evening, and though none but the leaders knew, when he started, where he was going.

Another example of swift work was given by the Klan in a Kentucky city. On the evening before an election the Klan suddenly decided to put up a candidate; there was one brief newspaper advertisement, but there were no meetings and no visible campaign. Yet of twelve thousand votes next day, this unknown man got seven thousand!

Thus, with autocratic generalship, military discipline and a perfect contact system with obedient forces, the Klan is able to plan campaigns without possibility of the plans becoming known, to act absolutely as a unit, to change instantly and without confusion when necessary and to throw its whole strength, without warning and in an hour's time against whatever objective is chosen. Few generals have had a more perfect fighting machine.

But this is only a part of the Klan's strength in action; probably less than half. Its greatest power comes from secrecy, and this is so tremendously effective that it is easy to see why it holds to secrecy in the face of all criticism. It more than doubles the chance that the Klan will accomplish the things it has set out to accomplish.

Dr. Evans spoke of some of these advantages in one of his talks with me.

"A force which is in the open and can be seen and calculated is far less feared by a corrupt official or an anti-American propagandist than one which he can not see," the Wizard said. "It is far more difficult and less comfortable to undertake a conspiracy against good government or against Americanism if the conspirator has no means of knowing that the first man in whom he confides his plans may not be a Klansman.

"These advantages are very real and assist in carrying out the Klan's ideals. In an open democracy they would not be necessary and might be classed as unfair. In the present condition of the country, when it is necessary to combat organizations using these and even worse methods, it would be folly to surrender any advantage. When the time comes that the organizations referred to abandon their secrecy, the Klan will also willingly abandon its secrecy."

These fighting values of secrecy are worth looking into, as they are among the Klan's most dangerous and effective weapons. The Imperial Wizard did not mention them at all, nor say all that is worth saying of any of them. A study of the Klan at work shows at least seven different advantages which it gains in this way.

First is the fact that it can strike in the dark. There is no warning before the blow falls, no certain knowledge of what is behind it. It is seldom possible to say with assurance, even that it was the Klan that acted; it is never possible to know what men are responsible. A blow so struck is doubly effective against the man hit; it is bewildering to the onlookers.

In the second place the Klan by this means is able to claim all successes and to deny any failures. If the blow lands it can take the credit, but if it misses, it is never known that anything was attempted or, if known, the Klan can deny responsibility. In regard to things which really are accomplished the advantage is the same. The Klan can take credit for actions which the community approves or fears, and deny blame for those which have not worked out to its advantage. Thus it is able to build up an aura of success, infallibility and social service which may or may not be justified, but is never quite so well justified as appears.

THE CHALLENGE OF THE KLAN

A third great advantage of secrecy is the one first mentioned by Dr. Evans, that it confuses the enemy. A man who contemplates a fight against the Klan does not know how great may be the force against him nor how to calculate his chances. It may have five members or five hundred and all the instinct against jumping in the dark will make men keep peace with it if they can. When it comes to an actual struggle it has all the advantages so well demonstrated by Gideon's band against the hosts of the enemies of Israel. The Klan might be beaten often if its foes kept their nerve, but very few men do keep their nerve against hard-hitting specters, for, as an infantry officer once told me, a single hidden rifleman can demoralize a company, when a hundred known opponents can not. The Klan keeps its sharpshooters hidden.

The Klan's ability to get information is secrecy's fourth great advantage. The benefit is not only the one mentioned by Dr. Evans, that no one can be sure there is not a Klansman included in the most carefully guarded plot who will lay all the details before the Klan officials, though this is disheartening enough. But the great advantage is that there is likely to be some Klansman who will get hold of the most carefully guarded secrets of any kind, and with men everywhere the high Klan officials are able to run down with very little trouble, whatever information they desire, whether secret or not. The fact that the membership is secret makes it impossible to guard against this.

I have had some contact with the espionage and secret service systems of three great governments, and it seems to me that the Klan's is the best of them all. In my talks with Klan officials I have been astonished at the extent and detail of their information. It covers every man with whom they may have business, from presidents to bootleggers, and apparently includes an actually complete record of each. It covers also political and business deals, plots, logrollings, plans, performances, past, present and to come. It seems on the whole as accurate as such secret information ever is, though there are serious inaccuracies. The Klan has a great bureau which collects, sorts, codifies and prepares all this material.

This kind of information is a tremendous weapon. The power which it might give the Klan over any man with a past, even over any man who does not want the affairs of his whole life and business made public at any given moment, is almost incalculable, though I have not heard a whisper that it has ever been used in this blackmailing way. It is also of great value in allowing the Klan to act with uncanny accuracy, and this seems to have been the chief use made of it, so far. And the very fact of its existence does have a blighting effect on all kinds of opposition.

All these things combine to give the fifth advantage

—terror. It may not include fear of physical force, but it is none the less real. Where the Klan is active there is often actual panic among opponents. It is like the fear of ghosts; men who would stand willingly against visible heavy odds are demoralized by a vague, unformed, unseen, intangible specter, armed with unknown weapons and unguessed knowledge and clothed with a reputation for ruthless power and unvarying success.

The sixth advantage is that secrecy protects individual Klansmen against reprisals. They can not be located, therefore can not be hurt. Thus the best known method of weakening an organized enemy—"sniping" the weaker members—is impossible against the Klan. Any blow which is struck in return must be aimed at the Klan as a whole.

And when such a blow is aimed, usually there is nothing there to take it. This is the final and greatest advantage of secrecy. It is almost impossible to hit back at the Klan except through general legislation and court actions such as have been attempted so often —and so fruitlessly. Those whom the Klan attacks can never know when or where or how or against whom to launch their counter-attacks. They must remain forever on the defensive, which is the surest road to final defeat.

One more advantage of secrecy—not of immediate fighting value but of great help to the Klan as a whole —should be mentioned. This is that secrecy goes far toward preventing individual Klansmen from exploiting themselves, from using the Klan to further their own ambitions. This keeps the Klan campaign and purposes unified, prevents perversion of aims and waste of strength in side-issues. Such things do occur, of course, but the rule of secrecy greatly limits them and the weaknesses that come from them.

There are two other great elements of strength in the Klan in action, neither directly due either to secrecy or organization. One is the careful spread of information among members; "education" as the leaders call it. This information is not always correct, but it always supports Klan purposes. The Klansmen are given reports about men and events from all over the country—reports that smack of "inside dope"— which strengthen their purposes and justify their actions. This helps much toward unity, intensity and effectiveness.

Last and by no means the least is that the Klansmen themselves believe not only in the righteousness of their cause and its methods, but in its actual success. They believe that they are doing the things they set out to do, and can do them everywhere if they will hold together and take enough trouble. Thus they have the *morale, esprit de corps, éclat* of a victorious army with all their incalculable value.

There is room for only one example of this belief that success is being won; an excerpt from a letter written by a clergyman in a state where the Klan has been heard from so little that few people know of its existence there. Since I have no personal knowledge of the facts, I suppress the names, and give the letter merely to show how Klansmen believe the Klan is winning.

"For two decades," this minister writes, "Bishop Blank has held the state in the hollow of his hand by cleverly manipulating the Catholic vote. Those ballots have been handed to any one who would be most convenient and accommodating to Rome. But when the Klan came, matters immediately changed and the haughty Bishop received what rightfully belonged to him and the church and nothing more. You are doubtless familiar with what has been done in this city in a political way. Senator Richard Roe has been the leader in the movement to take the management of city and state affairs out of the Bishop's hands and place it in the keeping of all the people. This great work will certainly result in his being chosen governor in the November election. *Rome's political machine here has been wrecked.*"

So we find the Klan going into action with an amazing array of the accouterments of success: unity, secrecy, immunity to reprisal, the ability to inspire panic, wide information and faith in victory. With such equipment it is no wonder that it is accomplishing much, it is expecting to do much more, that it is drawing increasing numbers into its march and that its leaders see no limits to what may be done. Given another year or two at the present rate of growth, and the possibilities of its power stagger the mind.

This summary has taken no consideration of the fairness or viciousness of these elements of the Klan strength. It will be observed that none of these methods is illegal, that many are of the kind that are highly praised when found in organizations which we happen to approve, and that the worst of them are measures which are always held to be justified in warfare, no matter how despicable they may be in themselves. The Klan practises espionage, a sort of mental terrorism, a secret propaganda, attack from ambush. These are not new methods; every combatant uses them in war-time and they are not unknown to political and other organizations in this country, even in peace.

Judgment on them must depend on one's judgment as to the motives and purposes of the Klan. The methods are undeniably dangerous, they are unfair in all ordinary circumstances as Dr. Evans himself practically admitted. The Klan's justification is that war is necessary to protect and save Americanism, that such methods are required, and that the Klan is not the first to use them but has adopted them as the Allies adopted poison gas, since it has merely done the same things that are constantly being done by those whom it classes as enemies of the country. From this point of view its only fault is that it has done them better! It can claim also in mitigation that its own aims are open, while those of the anti-American bodies and workers are not.

If one agrees with the Klan that the situation is serious enough to call for a vigorous campaign along the lines of the Klan programme, then, it would seem, the organization and strategy it uses can not be seriously condemned, although they may cause great misgivings. But it follows also that they must be abandoned at the earliest possible moment, and one must believe that the danger is very great and very imminent to justify such methods even temporarily. It will be recalled from Dr. Evans' statements that he admits both judgments.

CHAPTER IX

THE SPECTER'S HEAVY HAND

THE Ku Klux Klan, whatever its faults, has one quality much praised by moralists. It gets action, wasting no time in vain words. In fact there is reason to believe that this admirable trait is the chief cause for the tremendous hostility it has aroused. Most of us endure very calmly all sorts of opinions or projects so long as they remain safely elocutionary. It is when the ideas come to life and bite some one that loud anathemas arise. The Klan certainly gets this much tribute from its enemies; a tribute that would hardly be paid if it confined its activities to adopting resolutions.

The effect the Klan produces on the community is the final test of the power and success of the movement, and to a large extent of its justification. Its whole purpose is to get things done; it makes almost no attempt to spread ideas outside its own actual or prospective members. Its internal discussions are no disputations over theory. Often it can not even state its own case clearly. Everything is aimed toward the single purpose of changing our individual, community and national lives. For this the Klan has built up its autocratic generalship, its solidly welded unity, its secrecy, its terrorism and its intense emotionalism. And because of all this heaped-up power and this singleness of purpose, the impact, when the Klan does strike, is terrific, even though it is often invisible.

In its actual methods of reforming society, as well as in the general system and strategy)described in the previous chapter, the Klan is seldom seen and never heard. It is often, perhaps usually, impossible even to know for a certainty that it is the Klan that acted, no matter how evident the results may be. The thing is done—that is about all that can be known in any one case. It is a heavy hand that strikes, yet it is as if a specter held the weapon and directed the blow. Only through comparing what has happened in many different places can the methods by which the Klan acts be traced with any degree of accuracy.

It should be understood that these methods and, indeed, most of the instances given of their operation, can not be definitely proved to have any connection with the Klan. They are too well concealed. Thus this report is based on "general information and belief." But because so many similar situations appear wherever the Klan exists and seldom appear elsewhere, the connection between the two must be assumed, even if it can not be proved.

The means by which the Klan acts are ordinary

enough in life both in America and elsewhere; most organizations and most persons use them constantly. They are deadly in the Klan's hands merely because of the power and skill with which it uses them—like David and his sling.

There is, for example, the sense of a lurking menace which the Klan always manages to create in the popular mind. There is doubtless a menace, but the Klan "bluffs" the public far beyond its real strength or its real ruthlessness, just as we all try more or less to make those with whom we deal feel that we are a bit stronger or a bit more determined than we actually are. The Klan "works its bluff" to perfection. The ordinary citizen comes to believe that it is a cruel and determined monster of unknowable strength, working by diabolic methods, through invisible agents, guided by infernal acumen and able to hurt him through every means that a man dreads. Since so much is unknown, his fears are always exaggerated.

There may not be, and in most Klan towns there never has been, an actual demonstration of force. But unless they are themselves attacked men do not care to become involved in a trouble they can not measure. This holds the bulk of any community neutral and leaves those whom the Klan does attack unsupported and undefended. Klan officials deny that they try to terrify people; I can not say that they do, but this condition of being "bluffed to a standstill" is the first fact to be noted in any Klan community, and so far as my experience goes is never missing.

This fear of the Klan is often so effective that no further weapon is called for; a decree has only to be issued to be obeyed. Probably a great many decrees which do not come from the Klan are also issued and obeyed. But when there is resistance the Klan applies with scientific precision either social ostracism or a boycott, or both. After a single demonstration of these there is seldom need of further direct action, and usually none is taken unless for definite punishment or to drive some person out of the community.

Let me hasten to say that I am not accusing the Klan of illegal conspiracy in these measures. There is no order to Klansmen to ostracize or stop trading with the obnoxious persons; information is simply given that these persons are obnoxious. The distinction may seem small, but I believe this method has been declared legal in various cases where labor boycotts were involved. Klansmen are free to act on this information or not as they choose, but they all seem to choose to act. Let me quote Dr. Evans on this:

"I know of no case where speakers have advocated and pronounced official boycott. Where called to my attention and information is furnished, they will be summarily removed. It is contrary to law and in violation of the principles of the Klan. This refers to a specifically defined illegal boycott.

THE SPECTER'S HEAVY HAND

"As to the conferring or withholding of patronage by Klansmen because of various attitudes of business or professional men, that is a very different matter. Vocational Klannishness—in other words the practise of doing business with other Klansmen—is a tenet of the Klan as of every other fraternity, including the Rotary Club and the Kiwanis Club, which specifically means 'we trade.' It is to be expected that in cases where people are hostile to the Klan or are guilty of un-American practises or of serious misconduct, Klansmen will withhold patronage as individuals. If it becomes generally known that certain firms, for example, have discharged employees for no other reason than that they are Klansmen, it would naturally react against that firm with other Klansmen. It is also natural that Klansmen and sometimes local Klans having information of this kind should disseminate it. But a Klansman is always free to act as he pleases on such information."

The first move of a Klan when it starts to clean up a town seems to be among its own members. It makes them behave; several have complained to me that since joining they were no longer allowed to drink! The Klan has rules of conduct and a system of trial and punishment inside itself which are most effective. Nor are the crimes it punishes only those against fellow-members. There is little doubt that the level of conduct is raised among men who join.

The sections of the Constitution covering this matter of Klan crimes show why this is so. They are as follows:

OFFENSES AND PENALTIES

ARTICLE XX

Section 1. Offenses against this Order shall be divided into two classes—major offenses and minor offenses.

Section 2. Major offenses shall consist of (1) treason against the United States of America; (2) violating the oath of allegiance to this Order or any supplementary oath or obligation thereof; (3) disrespect of virtuous womanhood; (4) violation of the Constitution or the laws of this Order; conspiring against the interest and prosperity of this Order or any Klansman in any way or being a party thereto, or being a party to any move, conspiracy or organization whose existence is antagonistic or injurious to or is an imitation of this Order; whose name, style or title is a colorable imitation of this Order; swearing allegiance to or otherwise become a citizen or subject of any nation, government or institution of any nature or classification whatsoever, or any ruler or potentate, prince or person of any court whatever that is foreign to or is inimical to the government of the United States of America and its established institutions, or aiding or abetting such government, nation, institution, ruler, potentate, prince or person against the interest, well-being or dignity of the United States of America or the distinctive institutions of its government; violating the by-laws of a Klan of this Order; excessive or habitual drunkenness; drunkenness or the drinking of intoxicating liquor or entering a klonklave in an intoxicated condition; the habitual use of profane language or vulgarity during a klonklave or during an assembly of Klansmen just prior thereto; (5) being responsible for the polluting of Caucasian blood through miscegenation, or the commission of any act unworthy of a Klansman; (6) the repeated commission of a minor offense shall in itself constitute a major offense.

Section 3. MINOR OFFENSES. Minor offenses shall consist of drunkenness, drinking of intoxicating liquor during a klonklave or on the premises thereof, entering a klonklave in an intoxicated condition, use of profane language or vulgarity during a klonklave or in an assembly of Klansmen just prior thereto, or committing any other act which might operate against the best interest of the Klan or Klansmen, refusal or failure to obey the mandates, rules, edicts and orders of the Exalted Cyclops of the Klan, or the failure or refusal on the part of any Klansman, upon demand by the Exalted Cyclops, to respond to any summons issued by him, unless he has a providential excuse; or failure or refusal to surrender his credentials when called for by the Exalted Cyclops.

THE CHALLENGE OF THE KLAN

Section 4. PENALTIES: All offenses enumerated above under the head of major offenses shall be tried and penalities assessed by the Tribunal hereinafter provided for. All offenses enumerated as minor offenses shall be heard and determined and penalties assessed by the Exalted Cyclops of the Klan. Penalties shall be of four classes, as follows: 1, Reprimand; 2, Suspension; 3, Banishment; 4, Extreme Penalty—banishment forever, and there shall be added thereto complete ostracism in any and all things by each and every member of this Order.

The second move is against outsiders, usually against men or women who have offended against the Klan's moral ideas. These are rather strict, being set by the same literal-minded, church-going class of decent people who have given us prohibition, who demand strict observance of the Sabbath, and who have no sympathy for any sexual indulgences. Often the victims are Catholics, Jews and aliens, but I have learned of no case in which there was not some definite charge of misconduct against them, as well as the general fact of their faith or race.

Bootleggers seem to be the favorite objects of attack; the Klan crusade against them at Herrin, Illinois, has been widely advertised and has been initiated in hundreds of towns. I find that in some dozen places from which I have information the price of liquor—the best gauge of law enforcement—has

206

risen from two to five hundred per cent. since the Klan took hold. Bootleggers may always be counted among the Klan's chief enemies. Dope-peddlers come in for attention, social vice is censored, grafting officials are taken care of, places of amusement regulated, unfair business dealings punished.

There is also much effort put into regulating personal conduct. I have stories of Klan influence being brought to bear on men who maintained illicit relations with women, who failed to support their families, drank or gambled too heavily, or in general "acted scandalously." The great bulk of this private reformation has to do with the cruder instances of sexual irregularity.

With most of these a warning, backed by the individual's own fear of the Klan, brings prompt reformation. When this fails pressure is applied, running through ostracism and boycott up to measures which in extreme cases drive the culprit into exile. The whole procedure can be illustrated by a single case, which is typical in that even the victim himself does not know certainly that his enemy is the Klan. It occurred early in 1924 in an eastern state, in one of those communities where the original inhabitants have inbred, fallen rather low, and dropped much of their pretense to morality. The reformers seem to be newcomers, backed by a few of the better bred old residents.

In the town which is the center of this community

a young man who is steady, hard working and fairly trustworthy, was living with a notoriously vicious woman. He was called to the telephone one evening and advised to leave her. The speaker argued at some length, explained that the example was bad, made the proper bringing up of children more difficult, and so forth. A week was allowed for action. At the end of that time a second brief warning was given, in which he was told that he would regret it if he was not rid of the woman in three days.

He kept her. On the fourth day he lost his job, for plausible reasons. The next day his landlord demanded an exorbitant raise in rent, for plausible reasons. He found that supplies were cut off; the milkman disappeared, the butcher's wagon failed to stop, and when he went to the stores he could get little attention—all for plausible reasons. Shortly after this, some of the stores told him flatly that his trade was not wanted. By the end of the week only one man would sell him food and this grocer—who had defied a telephone warning—was brought into line within the next week by the loss of nearly seventy per cent. of his trade.

The fight—if it can be called that—was over inside two weeks. The young man moved to a hovel some miles in the country, where friends were at hand. As this is written he is still out of work, living precariously on his friends' charity. Such further orders as have come over the telephones of that town have been instantly obeyed.

As an example of the use of the boycott in punishment, let me submit a list read at a meeting of the Klan in northern Ohio. It is written from memory and incomplete, but nearly enough exact to do for illustration. The names used here are of course fictitious. The speaker made no recommendation for action. He said, in effect:

"I wish to tell you some of the things your fellow-townsmen have done.

"The Elite Clothing Store sells half-cotton goods as pure wool.

"Arthur Fredericks, a doctor, is a dope user.

"John Polaris, a restaurant keeper, has been trafficking in women.

"Michael O'Flynn's soft drink parlor sells white mule.

"Walter Peters got a slice of that paving contract graft.

"Jim Brady, the cigar store man, has a starving wife in Omaha and has been making love to some girls here.

"Benjamin Strauss, the dry goods man, underpays his girls, and besides expects too much of them—you understand.

"Fred Preston's drug-store will give you the white stuff if you know the sign.

THE CHALLENGE OF THE KLAN

"John Barton joined the Klan just to get trade, and has been turned out."

And so on. It was an amazingly inclusive list and on its face showed neither race nor religious persecution. Klansmen there boast that more than sixty men and firms have been put out of business in that town for reasons such as these. It seems to work, for when the crowd got back to town late that night, not one went into Polaris' restaurant, though it was empty, they were hungry and some had to wait an hour to be served in other restaurants.

It should be observed that in such cases the effective strength of the boycott is far greater than the Klan membership. This is due to the spread of information —or rumors—about the man under attack, which brings in the support of many outsiders. It may be mere back-fence gossip, but it is more likely "whispering campaigns" developed to a fine art.

A final method used by the Klan in its clean-up is to lay information before the regular officers of the law, and to bring pressure to bear on them. This is the only means officially sanctioned by the Klan of affecting conduct, and is being used increasingly. The fund of information the Klan gathers makes it extremely effective, both in inducing the officers to act and in providing evidence for them to act on. It is wholly commendable.

In some parts of the country there is a strong belief

that even though night-riding has stopped, the Klan is still guilty of murder. Since no case of the kind has ever been proved, it is added that if the man detailed as executioner is ever brought to trial, the Klan through its influence with officers and juries sees that he is acquitted. I can not do more than report this belief. These rumors are to be expected in any section where shooting is common, and are current concerning any powerful local organization. I have been in places where the Masons, the Odd Fellows and the Elks were similarly accused, and on plausible evidence. Possibly they are sometimes true, though I have never heard of one being proved. If any Klan has been guilty it has been successful in escaping justice. But if the charges are true they affect only about a quarter of the present Klan, for in the territory where the bulk of its strength now lies I have not found even a whisper of violence.

The question, however, of how much officers of the law favor Klansmen in places where the organization is strong, is a serious and universal one. Most people believe that there is little chance of a Klansman ever being brought to justice in a Klan-ruled community. This belief has somewhat weakened since Philip Fox was convicted of murder in Atlanta; incidentally the growth of the Klan jumped after this happened. The Klan's opponents who had confidently predicted that Fox would be freed and had emphasized the control the Klan was supposed to have over

Georgia courts, found themselves caught in their own argument.

My own opinion—I have met Fox and must admit a liking for him—is that the Klan does not control the Georgia courts, and also that it made no improper effort to have Fox acquitted, but merely to see that he was fairly tried. I do know that his friends hoped he would be found insane—a plea frequent enough outside Klan circles.

Dr. Evans declares that the Klan does not try nor wish to control or influence any court. As has already been pointed out he says the Klansman's oath will not prevent his telling the truth about his membership in the Klan or about anything else, for that matter.

In spite of this attitude and some vigorous efforts to convince law officers of it, there is evidence that in Klan counties it is difficult to get convictions of Klansmen. One instance occurred at Macon, Georgia, where several men were on trial for night-riding. The first man up was acquitted, but when the second man was arraigned, the Grand Dragon sent a message which was read to the jury, that the Klan did not support him nor wish anything but justice. On the same evidence as in the first case, the jury hung. It seems clear that in sending that message the Grand Dragon admitted his belief that the jury in the first trial had been swayed by fear of the Klan.

There were similar cases in Tulsa, Oklahoma, after

the Klan strength there became manifest, and I was told that no Klansman has been convicted of anything since the Klan-supported administration came into power. This is hardly a record to be accounted for by the virtue of Klansmen. There can be no doubt, too, that officials who owe their election to Klan support will be inclined, in common gratitude, to give Klansmen all the favors their consciences will allow; some official consciences are very elastic, and the gratitude of politicians is usually highly developed, since re-election depends on it.

So there is little doubt that the law in Klan communities is likely to favor Klansmen—as it does certain other classes in other places. Political influence over courts and law officers in this country has been suspected and has sometimes been proved. But this is an evil of popular government, not chargeable to the Klan unless it puts pressure on the law officers, a matter almost impossible to prove.

On the whole there is a good deal to show that the general effect of the Klan crusades has been good. The circuit judge quoted in a previous chapter told me that in his district the Klan had done "substantial justice"; an Oklahoma judge confirmed this. Both said that the general morality and decency had been' improved. My own observations agree with this. This judgment is, of course, entirely apart from any question of the good or evil of the methods employed.

The same thing is true of crimes, even of crimes of violence, in spite of the general belief about the Klan. The Klan information bureau has statistics which show a decrease in crime in the states where the Klan is strong. Governor Walton of Oklahoma, at the same time that he was attacking the Klan, boasted of a fifty per cent. decrease in crime in the state. Statistics from either source are subject to challenge, of course; but it is certain that lynching, which might be supposed a peculiarly Klannish crime, has decreased more than half in the year of the Klan's great growth. There are several instances where Klans have helped sheriffs prevent mob violence.

While on the subject of crime it may be well to give Dr. Evans' statement about the Mer Rouge affair, since that is often cited as a complete condemnation of the Klan. This is the first official statement that has come from a Klan leader on the subject, and denies both that Klansmen were guilty or that the Klan refused to help the prosecution.

"The true story of Mer Rouge has not been told," he said. "That is about all the Klan knows about it. It does not know who were guilty nor of what they were guilty. It does know that the prosecution of the case has been proceeding on a wrong theory and against the wrong men. It has been accused of not aiding the prosecution; it has had no information that it could give. Some such information, as yet unverified, has recently come to us. If that information proves correct it will be given to the authorities and the truth will be learned at last."

In all this Klan crusading there has been much talk of abuse of innocent people, and of punishment inflicted for the mere fact of opposing the Klan when there were no charges of crime or misconduct. Here again the situation is foggy. Undoubtedly there have been cases of mob violence when there was no least justification for it, and many of these have occurred at times and places where the Klan was active. The Klan's denial of responsibility in such cases is not convincing, since the conditions which make such outrages possible, if not the outrages themselves, are due to the Klan. In fairness it must be added that the proportion of these cases to the total activities of the Klan is very small, and that most of them, that I have heard of, took place prior to the Evans reforms.

One more point: Dr. Evans and the other leaders are now trying to stop "meddling" with the private conduct of people, as they have stopped night-riding. The rule has been laid down that the Klan shall never take direct action, and that no case shall be acted upon except through the regular law officers under enacted statutes. Dr. Evans believes that "meddling" largely has been stopped, but I am forced to disagree with him. The cases I have cited are all recent and in northern and eastern states. There is reason to believe that the evil is decreasing considerably, but it is far from dead.

THE CHALLENGE OF THE KLAN

It will be observed that all these methods of the Klan, including those disapproved by the leaders, are entirely legal, except the doubtful and unproved cases of actual violence, or of intimidation of legal officers. It is hard to attack these methods in the abstract, even on moral grounds, since they are, in the last analysis, nothing but an organized exercise of the right to like whom we please, associate with whom we please, and do business where we please. We have heard a good deal lately about the immense good to be accomplished by public opinion and "social and economic pressure." Here we have it; the Klan has made it a science!

The objection, of course, is that this is private justice, outside the law, without trial or the chance for defense. True; but the same can be said of the personal verdicts and preferences which each of us passes and enforces daily. As to the use of rumors, we all act constantly on unproved rumors, and make people suffer for them. The Klan has organized both rumor and opinion and it would seem at first that there could be no very well-founded objection nor very strong condemnation for merely doing better than others, things that we all do.

Yet there is objection. Almost everywhere that the Klan appears there soon develops very bitter opposition. This comes not merely from the vicious and criminal classes, hit in the reform campaigns. That is to be expected and is a good symptom. It comes

also, of course, from Catholics, Jews and aliens and
has apparently resulted in strengthening the unity of
these groups, thus producing an effect directly oppo-
site to that at which the Klan aims. I say "apparently" because while there are many statements that
this is the case I have been unable to obtain from the
Knights of Columbus or the B'nai Brith answers to
registered letters asking for the facts. But this opposition also was to be expected, and in so far as parts
of these groups have been working for class or anti-
American interests, it is also wholesome.

Entirely apart from this, however, there is strong
opposition to and intense feeling against the Klan
among those same native white Protestants to whom
it tries to appeal. Much of this, to be sure, is based
on misinformation about what the Klan actually is
and wants, and some of it on snap judgments, or
prejudices inherited from the Civil War days. But
a considerable number of bitter opponents of the Klan
are not accounted for in any of these ways, and the
reasons for their attitude are rather obscure, since it
seems to be based only in small part on charges that
the Klan has been unjust in individual cases, and is
frequently accompanied by the admission that it has
done good. The reasons usually given are vague and
not fundamental; disapproval of secrecy, of espionage,
or the statement that "nobody's got any business doing
such things."

There are many people, of course, who hate the

Klan merely because they fear it, and never acknowledge that reason. But the real cause of the most serious opposition seems to me to lie in the complaint against meddling. On analysis it shows three sound reasons against the Klan methods, even against the modified methods the leaders are trying to enforce. The first is, that public opinion and our individual attitude toward obnoxious persons are often unjust and unfair, imply a right to judgment which can not be well maintained, and are tempered in their effect by varying opinions in the community as a whole. These evils, overlooked and ignored in ordinary social relations, become magnified and self-condemning when they appear on a large and organized scale.

In the second place there is a vast difference between pressure applied by the community as a whole and a similar pressure applied, even in the same ways, by a part of the community which has arrogated full power to itself.

In the third place there is no safeguard that the power of the Klan will not be perverted at any moment to all kinds of personal desires—spite, jealousy, revenge, ambition or plain meanness.

The objections to the Klan on the ground of secrecy and espionage are loud but very often do not ring true. Most of the objections I have heard have come from men who themselves belong to organizations more or less secret and more or less accustomed to use espionage. They are anxious for laws which will stop the Klan from using those weapons, but balk when any attempt is made to provide laws which will stop all organizations from using them. This probably accounts for the futility of all anti-Klan laws so far passed. There are, of course, a few men who are clear-sighted and public-spirited enough to see these things as evils in themselves. Many of them are fighting the Klan, but they do not single it out for attack to the exclusion of other bodies.

At any rate, the opposition is there. In some places it has divided quiet communities into hostile factions. In others it is at present hidden, held down by fear of the Klan, but ready to spring into action if ever that fear dies. The Klan, I believe, will be stunned to find how great a baying will arise at its first sign of weakness. The storm which followed the collapse of the Know-nothings made their name a hissing for two generations, and the Klan will suffer no less. This suppressed hatred also makes it certain that if the Klan does begin to break up, its fall will be even faster than its growth.

CHAPTER X

THE GIANT BEGINS TO RULE US

THE really vital strength, the true hope or menace of the Ku Klux Klan lies in politics. It is
there that it can produce the greatest effect, cause the
most stunning impact on our lives, exert the deepest
influence on the nation. Its social, economic and spiritual activities, its terrorism and boycotting and possible violence, are important enough in all conscience
and will make or break thousands of lives, but com-
pared to what it may do in politics they are trifles.
For through politics the Klan may rule America!

It has already started; it expects to make its rule
secure and as complete as it wishes in a single year!

This hope is no wild dream. In sober truth there
is a very fair chance that the Klan may succeed. It
will surely go far toward it, though just how far no
one can even guess till the smoke has blown away
after the November elections. But its success will
be startling unless there comes one of those miracles
which are always possible in politics but which almost
never happen. In fact, the chance for a sweeping

Klan victory—no matter which party wins—is about as good as the chance for Coolidge to be elected. This does not imply that he is the Klan candidate—it has not yet picked its man—but illustrates how well justified is its hope that it will win in the play of skill and run of luck in our great national game.

The Klan's political power is already large for, as was pointed out in the first chapter, it has elected men of its choice to controlling places in six states, has dominated the elections in half a hundred Congressional districts and has won complete victories in many hundreds of towns, counties and small cities, to say nothing of throwing the whole political world into a spasm. It has already shown power, in short, about three times that of the non-Partisan League and double that of the Populists in their best days.

But this is only the beginning. At the coming elections the Klan expects—not merely hopes but confidently expects—to win more than twenty states, most of the local elections inside those states and hundreds outside them.

This is far from impossible. The Klan's present political power was won with far fewer and far less well-disciplined members than answer its roll-calls to-day. Two years ago in the Congressional elections it had fewer than 200,000 votes. Last fall when it scored so heavily, it had about 3,000,000. To-day it has some 4,500,000 and by election time it confidently counts on having 12,000,000. This doubtless includes many unhatched chickens, but even if the Klan growth continues at the average rate of the last three months—and the rate has increased steadily during that time—it will have close to nine million! And nine million votes is more than a third of the largest vote ever cast. Cleverly used these votes can get almost anything. When we recall the influence that has been exerted by the two million German hyphenates or the three million Jews, the possible power of nine million Klansmen, or even of eight or seven or six or five, begins to be clear.

The Klan intends to win. Its leaders believe that a victory will give it freedom from the persecutions and prosecutions which have plagued it so far, give it a chance to consolidate its power and trim off its excrescences and make certain internal reforms they dare not yet attempt, and let it prove to the world the worth of its theories and its programme. More, they believe that they will have difficulty in even holding the organization together without a victory, and that it is absolutely necessary if they are to keep on growing. They realize, too, how fast their mushroom growth will crumble under any adversity. For all these reasons they are gambling heavily on this one card.

So they have focused all their efforts on politics. They do not admit it, but I am convinced that this is the true explanation of several of the present abuses in the Klan: the acceptance of riff-raff members, the carelessness about collecting dues and even initiation fees, the tolerance of grafters and self-seeking leaders in minor places. All will help until and at the election, therefore all will be tolerated until that time. Then the Klan can clean house!

This explains, too, the tremendous pressure behind the kluxing, which is absorbing most of the funds of the Order, the devotion of the great secret information service to the collection of political "dope," the transfer to Washington of most of the high executives (headquarters remains at Atlanta but little is done there) and the busy establishment of a Klan-controlled press and a dozen other lesser symptoms. If the Klan fails to achieve its political ambitions it will not be for want of using every ounce of strength it possesses.

So far as local elections and local governments are concerned the control which the Klan seeks is practically absolute; there are limitations on its national ambitions which will be explained in the following chapter. And in these local campaigns the chief difficulty that the Klan has and will have, is not so much with its opponents as inside its own ranks.

The most numerous of the various breeds of parasites with which the Klan is afflicted is composed of cheap politicians who seek a chance to get jobs or graft which they have been unable to reach in ordinary party politics, or to hold on to places or profits they are in danger of losing. Blatherskites, crooks, grafters, chronic kickers, chronic candidates, criminals de-

223

pendent on political pull, "has-beens" and all the flotsam of political life have grabbed at the Fiery Cross as a hope of salvation. They are so obstreperous, one political observer told me, that in his state the whole Klan movement was "an attempt of the political scrap-heap to seize the government." Along with these, too, there has gone into the Klan a swarm of fanatics and world-savers who are trying to get it to support every known crack-brained and half-baked reform. Witness the "monkey-bill" to prevent the teaching of evolution which was passed in Oklahoma with Klan support, and the attempt to suppress all private schools in Oregon.

These noisy and pestiferous members, however, do not represent either the great body of the Klan or its national leadership. They are apparently tolerated, as such are always tolerated in new political movements, for the sake of their votes. It was their presence in the Progressive Party, I believe, which inspired Roosevelt to coin the term "lunatic fringe." Certainly the Progressives gathered up a mighty following of them, and of the political hoboes as well.

In fact, there are many other ways in which the Ku Klux movement resembles the Progressive Party. It contains about the same basic elements of partly dissatisfied and partly idealistic middle-class folk, as well as the same fringes. Its gatherings have the same appearance and feeling. It is strong in about the same parts of the country, and it sings *Onward,*

Christian Soldiers just as indefatigably as the Bull Moosers did. It has much of the same naïve, inexperienced, youthful vigor.

All these conditions in the membership limit not only the programme of the Klan in politics, but also the demands it may make on candidates, bosses or men in office. Its political record so far shows that it has very largely respected these limits. It can seldom nominate its own man, for example, as that would aid one party or the other. It can not pick the men whom it is going to support on any party basis, but only on the basis of their ability and willingness to support the Klan programme, and their general fitness.

The church-going proclivity of most Klansmen makes personal character unusually important for candidates in Klan territory, and is likely to enforce more than usually decent administration from officials. It also gives the Klan a political morality rather above the average, which is no very great praise. There are cases, of course, as in other similar movements, when very decent citizens overlook all other qualifications in a candidate except his support of their pet ideas. This has caused some curious situations, such as those in the Anti-Saloon League Campaigns where the churches have united behind men who were complete scalawags except for their willingness to vote for prohibition.

The Klan will very naturally support Klansmen

225

where possible, but it has often refused to do this and has often voted for non-Klansmen (in at least one case for an anti-Klan man) when it thought them better, even against Klan members. But I have learned of no case where it gave support to a man who was not a native, white Protestant. It takes pains to see that there is at least *one* such in every political race.

When the Klan does move in politics, that is, when it takes a hand in the selection or election of candidates, or in influencing officials, it brings to bear a pressure such as almost no other organization, even one of the great parties, can apply. All its organized unity, all its ability to strike suddenly in the dark, all its secret information and its terrorism, are even more effective here than in ordinary life, for politicians are by nature a very timid tribe.) The Klan, too, can use not only this stunning political battle ax; it can add to that the whole social and economic power described in the last chapter. Political bosses, it is true, often use similar additional means of coercing candidates and officials, but few are ever able to do it with a tithe of the force, and none of them with the demoralizing terrorism, that the Klan commands.

In politics, as in boycotting, the Klan claims no actual control over its members. It does not officially tell them how to vote, any more than it tells them to withhold trade from a business man. It merely gives them information, sometimes advice, and they are

226

"free to act upon it as they see fit." It also "educates" them as to the desirability of acting on this information, tion and advice.

I asked Dr. Evans how far the Klan controls the political action of its members.

"None whatsoever, so far as actual control is concerned," he replied. "No obligation of a Klansman, nothing in his oath or understanding requires of him or contemplates that he shall accept the information and educational facts presented to him through the Klan, as final. The whole thought is to develop a mind that it will express itself through an electorate fully informed.

"The actual strength of the Klan," he went on, "depends upon the extent to which Klansmen have been educated to their duties as citizens and on how they respond to information given by Klan officials. This is always uncertain, but experience indicates that these are generally accepted and will be as long as they represent in the minds of the Klansmen themselves true American ideals. In the present state of public opinion this means that the Klan can profoundly influence results in twenty-one states."

There will be more states in the list before election.

So far as I can learn Dr. Evans is correct in saying that the Klan does not give orders, only information. Certainly it has such information to give, and takes great pains in putting it out. Since it is secret, it would easily be possible to give false information of a kind that might be exceedingly dangerous, but I can not find that it does so, at least as far as actual candidates are concerned.

I have learned of several instances in which it has circulated, just before an election, a report on candidates much like the reports put out by Citizens' Committees and similar bodies. I have seen one such and have information on others. They are all startlingly detailed, intimate and exhaustive, but rather amazingly fair. The one I saw was put on in Oklahoma in the heat of a bitter fight, but there was no trace of partisanship visible. It gave both the personal and political records of each man, his affiliations in business, society, religion and politics, and his relations with the Klan. I was particularly impressed with the fact that when a man had joined the Klan under circumstances which indicated that his purpose had been to get political support, that fact was indicated. In several such cases the advice was that he should be beaten. So far as I could judge by that report, it was a valuable and trustworthy guide for any voter.

Incidentally, even if the advice given is bad, the training given voters by this system is a very considerable service to the community. If the Klan should succeed in teaching its members to judge candidates on any other basis than that of "regularity" and back-scratching and pie-gathering ability, it would do much for the future of democracy.

The actual political attitude of Klansmen as I have

seen them appears to be much more docile and de-
pendent, however, than Dr. Evans declares. Even on
the night before election they are likely not to know
what they are going to do at the polls; they are
"waiting for the word." Possibly this is merely the
information and advice Dr. Evans described, but the
attitude was that of soldiers waiting for and ready
to carry out orders. So it seems that in political practise, as it was in the application of a boycott, it makes
little difference in results whether "the word" is a
command or a bit of information or advice.

There is, on the other hand, some doubt how far
the Klansmen will follow the lead given. In one case
in Oklahoma a Klansman and a man whom the Klan
opposed, running on the same ticket, finished only a
few votes apart. There have been other cases where
the apparent voting strength of the Klan was nil. But
these are exceptions, possibly due to lack of "education" or some more subtle factor; they do prove that
the Klansmen seem to feel under no obligation to
follow their leaders in politics beyond a point which
they—the individual Klansmen—determine for themselves. This is important in showing the limits of
the leaders' power.

However, in nearly ninety per cent. of the cases I
have been able to check, the Klan apparently has cast
a practically solid vote. This is increasingly true, and
the Grand Dragon of Oklahoma told me that by next
fall the entire membership would be educated, and

"ready and able to make proper use of information given them." Dr. Evans adds that the Klan usually casts more than its own vote.

"We have found by experience," he remarked, "that when a Klan issue is raised or when the Klan becomes active in a political campaign, the actual pro-Klan vote will be much larger than the numerical strength of the Klan itself and sometimes many times as large." It should be added that the Klan officials declare that the Klan itself has never been allowed to become an issue, or a Klansman to run as such, unless an attack had been made on it. I have not found a case in which this was not true.

When it comes to the actual power of the Klan in political action the fact that it is not a party, does not want full control of offices, and therefore does not need an actual plurality of votes, gives it great advantages in the fight for the results it does demand. It leaves room for deals; for politicians to submit and yet save their faces. And a minority, willing to swing to either party a solid block of votes, is in a far better position to get results than even a party majority would be. The Anti-Saloon League has given the most convincing proof of this. Such a body can threaten both sides, quite likely secure pledges or dictate nominations on both sides and be victorious whichever party wins. If either party or candidate balks, it can usually swing enough votes to insure defeat.

THE GIANT BEGINS TO RULE US

The political law on which this minority power—the power of any minority—is based, is the very A B C of American politics, yet so often forgotten that I may be pardoned for recalling it. It is that *control of one-half of the movable or floating vote in any electorate gives political control.* For example, in most elections the two great parties are fairly evenly balanced, party loyalty, to each party, holding something like forty per cent. of its voters. The election then will be decided by the remaining twenty per cent. or the largest fraction thereof, for any leader who controls one vote more than half of them can throw victory whichever way he pleases. The man who wins must take his orders from that leader after election, as he has taken them before election.

The actual figures vary, of course, but the fact always is that victory does not depend on winning a majority of the voters, but only a majority of those who are not party-bound. Hence it is that any small and compact minority is usually able to get what it wants. The Klan's strength is that it has gathered together such a minority.

But the Klan's weakness is in the one exception to this rule; rather in its corollary. This is that *the minority power fails as soon as there is formed another group, equally large, and determined to vote against the first group.* If the two balance, both can be ignored. In practise this seldom happens. Pro-Germans, for example, were long able to act as a unit, while the rest of us were divided over tariff, conservation, or some other issue. In most local politics the "liquor vote"—and to-day the "bootleg vote"—can easily win in any campaign which divides the electorate on any other issue. Our electorate has become full of minority groups for which there are no offsets; racial, religious, business, farming, labor or whatnot, each without any corresponding group of "antis." Politicians and office holders cater to them all; they must, for if one is lost there is nothing to take its place.

In the case of the Klan, however, this law of opposition groups works with full force. The Klan automatically raises up its opponents; more accurately it is an opposition group itself, its chief object being to strike at certain of the groups already active, so that its balancing blocs are ready made. Many politicians therefore believe that they can win by defying the Klan and rallying all these groups behind them. As this is written there are indications that the northern Democratic leaders—Murphy, Sullivan, Taggart and their allies—are preparing to do this. Their plan is certainly logical, for in the cities where their main strength lies the bulk of the vote is alien, Jewish and Catholic, and naturally anti-Klan. It is worth a smile in passing to note that most of the Klan leaders and probably a slight majority of their followers are Democrats.

This rallying of alien elements has been the means

of defeating nativistic movements several times since Jefferson first did it, shortly after 1800. The Democratic party did it in the 'forties, and again in the 'fifties against the Know-nothings. With our present large alien element—the last census showed nearly four and half million alien-born citizens of voting age to say nothing of the children of aliens and the native Jews and Catholics who will naturally take sides against the Klan—the Democrats are certain of success in many localities.

The evils of an election based on these group divisions are too obvious to need reciting. The possible result to government by an alien, anti-American alliance, is also clear.

When I pointed out to Dr. Evans that the Klan by uniting these groups was likely to insure not only its own defeat, but the defeat of the very principles of Americanism for which it is standing, he minimized the danger. He declared that the very characteristics which have prevented the different national and religious groups from becoming assimilated, would also prevent their joining for any effective action. This may be true in some ways, but there is plenty of evidence that they are willing to join, at least to beat the Klan.

It is in meeting this opposition that the Klan's secrecy comes to its highest value, for the alien groups can not unite against Klan candidates unless they know whom the Klan is supporting, and they are barred from uniting on openly alien candidates of their own, because of the certainty that this would drive all Americans into the Klan ranks, insuring its victory. So they must work on the defensive, also in secrecy. But they have not and can not possibly have the solid and effective organization of the Klan.

Their task then, is a difficult one. They must select their candidates from among men who may already be Klansmen, work with groups which may include Klan members, convince the Americans among their followers that the men so selected are good Americans and convince the alien groups that the same men are pro-alien. And they must determine from among all the various candidates offered, which ones are favorable to the Klan and concentrate opposition upon them.

The last problem is the most baffling, for the Klan will not label its candidates. It has learned that lesson already in elections where open Klan support has solidified opposition. To-day its candidates are, when it seems desirable, as secret as is its organization. In one recent case the Klan press openly attacked the very man for whom "the word" finally went out. This system is peculiarly effective in primaries where several candidates are running and will often nominate pro-Klan men on both tickets. It will not be needed in many places, of course. Probably in most sections where the Klan operates its strength will be so great that it can fight best in the open. But when the fight is made behind a hood, it will be baffling.

Nor is there much chance that the opposition can checkmate the Klan by finding out in advance what it intends to do. This could be done easily if the Klan plans had to be confided in advance to the whole membership, for a leak would be almost certain. But the Klan need take no such risk. With the members waiting for "the word," that word can be held back till the last moment, often till the last hour before the polls close, when it will be far too late for any opposition to act. The Klan's system of passing information has been perfected to a point where, I am assured, the entire membership can be reached in less than two hours after the machinery is started. There are over five thousand offices kept open day and night to make this possible.

Altogether it seems, in this very complex situation, that the great solidarity and the amazing perfection of the organization of the Klan give it the advantage. If it does get the nine million members it may reasonably expect, it would also have an advantage in numbers. With these advantages it is quite justified in believing that at least so far as local elections are concerned it can count on a very satisfying measure of success—very satisfying indeed.

The one thing that is clear, is that in the coming campaign there will be a mess of underground politics, hidden issues, hypocritical candidates, and general wool-pulling and lying such as the country has never seen. The blame for this at first thought rests on the Klan, which has caused the crisis. But in all fairness must we not go back to the politicians and the groups which for years have been dickering, openly and secretly, with other minority groups, by the same filthy methods? The political crimes committed at the demand of these groups have been so many and have become so notorious that they have automatically aroused opposition. Not all members of the race and religious groups belong to these voting blocks by any means, but the blocks are there and have been used in many vicious ways by unworthy leaders. The Klan in politics is the more or less accidental vehicle of the very natural attempt to thwart them.

CHAPTER XI

THE PLAN TO CAPTURE WASHINGTON

THE coming national election, unless very carefully laid plans of the Ku Klux leaders miscarry, will make the Klan masters at Washington, with all that implies both in our government and our national life. This is the most startling statement in all the story of the hooded order.

It expects to rule America, not only by controlling thousands of local governments, but from the very top down, by controlling the national government. It expects, as a result of the coming election, to have in Congress a clear majority of members in both houses who are in sympathy with its aims or at least willing to vote for its programme, and in the White House a president who will, at the very least, put no obstacle in the way of the Klan demands, and will appoint to office no man the Klan disapproves. Indeed, each man appointed may actually be a member and a willing servant of the organization!

Impossible, you say? Too sudden, too incredible! Here is another statement even more impossible and incredible: The Klan is very likely to succeed in doing just this very thing. On the basis of cold-blooded political calculation the Klan is at least as likely to win as is any one of the different presidential candidates now before the public; as likely to win as is either of the two big political parties! For the plans of the Ku Klux leaders go behind the detail of party victory, and can succeed whichever of the two wins. There are still many things that can defeat it, of course; it hasn't victory wrapped and tied up. But this thing is sure: in all the welter of issues and scandals and plottings which will come between now and November, the Klan is almost certain to have the greatest influence in deciding the result.

For in the election the Klan, as a mugwump minority solidly united and under military discipline, will exert a tremendous power. This will be subject, to be sure, to the offset of whatever union the anti-Klan groups may be able to effect. But remember that the Klan now has 4,500,000 members, that it is likely to have 9,000,000 and expects to have 12,000,000 by November. Then consider that in the presidential elections during the present century (doubling the figures before 1920 to allow for the doubled voting strength under woman suffrage) the average plurality of the winning party has been only a little over 3,500,-000 so that an average change of 1,800,000 votes would have changed every election. In many cases a change of 750,000 would have been enough!

THE PLAN TO CAPTURE WASHINGTON

Consider also that in most Congressional districts a majority of 10,000 is rare and that in normal years a plurality of 50,000 for a state ticket is high; that a shift of 5,000 in a Congressional district and of 25,000 in a state would far more often than not, have changed the result. Finally remember that this is a year when all politicians expect a close vote. While, of course, there would be cases in which the Klan vote would change pluralities without affecting the result, it is plain that if even a fraction of Klan members take its advice, and if it can escape solid and effective oppositions it may easily win overwhelmingly.

It is true that the ability of the Klan to wield almost its full strength in local elections must be heavily discounted, in considering state and national votes. In local elections party loyalty is comparatively weak, while in national campaigns it will have a powerful hold on all but the most ardent Klansmen. How far the Klan "education" will be able to swing the members in the partisan heat of a national campaign is a very doubtful question, and there has been no demonstration of strength along this line on which an answer might be based. Politicians and political observers disagree on the answer; most of them declare that the Klan can be safely defied, but few of them act that way. But after all discounts it seems safe to say that if the Klan can control a quarter of its nominal strength it can win in most places.

All this, however, does not mean that the Klan

intends or wants to rule the country in the full sense, in the sense in which a political party takes control. On the contrary; its aims are very strictly limited, at least for the time being. Dr. Evans states this position in two sentences which are apparently contradictory.

"The Klan is not in politics," he and other leaders have told me over and over and over. Yet he goes on: "It is clear that the Klan programme must result in political action and be carried out in no other way."

This is not actually a contradiction. His meaning is that the Klan works in politics not as a party but as a mugwump, non-partisan, opportunist band of guerrilla reformers. It does not want—at least not yet—the full responsibilities of government, it does not want to face the need of apportioning patronage, it does not wish to have to find solutions for all the controversial political issues or to try to unite its following on them, and finally, it does not have to hold its organization together, as a political party does, by the use of place, pork and pie.

What it does want is to get certain things done— a most unusual political purpose in these days; to free itself from government opposition, to put into effect its programme of native, white, Protestant Americanism, to make some general reforms and to be able to claim a victory. It is playing for results only, while the old political parties are playing chiefly for offices. In this sense the Klan is not in politics.

THE PLAN TO CAPTURE WASHINGTON

But the Klan must be able to control officials and legislature if it is to put into effect any of the policies on either its national programme or its local platforms, or even if it is to make more than a temporary success out of the minor victories it has so far achieved. In this sense it is most completely in politics.

This self-denying attitude toward spoils and absolute power is not due solely to virtue. It is forced by the very nature of the Klan itself, by the fact that the membership is almost equally divided between the Democrats and Republicans. The moment that any attempt is made to take up issues which have proved partisan or which are even outside the platform on which the Klan has been built and is united, the moment that its power is turned to picking plums, above all at the first suspicion that its leaders are favoring either party—at that moment its membership would be split into a dozen bickering factions and its power would vanish. The Klan may be able to win on its present limited programme, but it can not, on the basis of any development now in sight, attempt anything more.

This is true whether the leaders recognize it or not. If Dr. Evans and the rest ever do yield to the constant pressure and "broaden out" the Klan plans, there will be another story to tell—an obituary notice. Its dying struggles might, it is true, produce results in strange fields, but, until they begin the Klan can have almost no political effect outside its chosen ground.

There is proof of this in the fall of the Know-nothings, to revert once more to that ill-fated fore-runner of the Klan. The sudden collapse of that movement was directly due to the mistake of attempting too much. As long as the organization remained secret and stuck to its own issues, it grew rapidly and wielded a mighty power. But the early successes went to the heads of the leaders and they came into the open as the American Party. For a year or two their power did increase, but by that time the seeds of trouble had germinated and ripened. Internal jealousies had festered, the attempt to graft on new issues had split off large sections, the desire for offices, the disputes over patronage and over compromises made to gather more votes, all took the life out of the original purposes. In the end an effort to straddle on the slavery issue, in an attempt to save votes, gave the death blow.

The movement would have been destroyed just as surely, however, whichever way it turned. The mistake was in getting into a position where it was forced to take a stand on any issue other than the one which had built it up, in forgetting that a movement based on one strong idea will be cut in two as soon as another strong idea is foisted into its counsels.

The more important of the Klan leaders recognize

this limitation, and have no desire to attempt to break away from it.

"If the Klan should ever make the fatal mistake of identifying itself with either party," Dr. Evans told me, "or with any cause except the fundamental issue of Americanism, it would invite division in its own ranks, destroy its own power and insure its own dismemberment."

Many Klansmen, however, even many of the lesser leaders, either do not see this or else are willing to ignore it for selfish reasons. Both the fanatics and the grafters are continually urging a diversion of strength to side-issues, and the struggle with these members demands much of the strength of the national officers, and gives the best reason possible for the autocratic and centralized control of the Klan under which these fanatics and grafters can be kept in check.

The actual voting strength of the Klan, great as it is, is only a part of the political power through which the Order is likely to accomplish its purposes. As great, if not greater, is the effect it can have privately, on candidates, on officials after they are elected and above all on bosses. These politicians, of whatever grade, can not tell how many votes the Klan might cast, they can not by any means be sure of an offsetting support if they antagonize the Klan, and they are open to the non-political pressure which the Klan can apply so effectively. Their easiest course by far will always be to fall in with the Klan demands. This form of terrorism in politics, or threat of reprisal combined with promise of reward, is a common feature of our political maneuvering, but the Klan can use it with unprecedented force.

It is already doing so; I have not yet met a single minor politician who is willing to speak openly against the Klan, and except for a few of the Democratic leaders and Col. Roosevelt, Jr., there is no recent record of any of them taking such a stand, though it was fashionable enough two years ago. The success of the Klan in so many local elections and the greater threat behind it to-day have upset the calculations of politicians everywhere and have thrown local posses in many places into a truly demoralized state of mind.

"You talk about the Klan terrifying folks," an Imperial officer said. "We don't aim to, except one bunch—the politicians. We do that thing. They're scared senseless right now, big ones as well as little ones. They don't know which end they're standing on, and they duck every time any one says 'Klan.' They're scared, terrified, paralyzed, buffaloed, licked!"

This is quite true. Thousands of them are in a state such that if the Klan offers them salvation on any terms they will seize it gratefully. There is, for instance, the case of a man who for a generation has ruled half a state by the good old system of controlling nominations in both parties, and then allowing the voters to worry about which of his pets they shall elect. Last fall he woke up the day after election to

find that both of his hand-picked beauties had been
snowed under by a man whose name he had not even
heard. His bewilderment and distress were piteous.
He is still in a daze, as if the sun had risen in the
west, the United States Government had gone bank-
rupt and fire had turned cold, all at once. He will
listen very, very carefully to such advice and hints as
the Klan will presently give him about delegates to
the national convention and next fall's candidates. He
is one of a great host.

The Klan system is just as effective where there
are rival bosses or unbossed rival candidates, either
in the election or the primaries. Each knows that to
win he must have a few dozen or hundred or thousand
votes in addition to his regular strength, and he must
hold all that strength. To each of these the Klan
goes, saying in effect:

"We control a large number of votes. We won't
tell you how many; you can do your own guessing.
But some of them you have counted in your own support and some are against you. We can throw the
whole block either way. We also know many things
about your private affairs, and have influence with
many of your business customers and associates.
Here, then, is a pledge that will satisfy us. Sign on
the dotted line."

How many will dare refuse? And of those who do
dare, how many will the Klan be able to beat? These
are the questions that must be answered before

one can estimate the Klan's chances of victory this fall.

Only a partial answer is possible now. In local elections where the party loyalty is weak and the national issues do not enter, the system should work almost perfectly, for the reasons already given, until or unless the opposition not only unites but finds out what to do. This system has resulted in the hundreds of victories already mentioned, and will undoubtedly win thousands more.

Nationally, it will work far less perfectly. In as far as the Klan can work in the primaries and conventions of both parties, and succeed in choosing both candidates, it will succeed completely. This will happen in a good many cases. It will certainly put not a few Klan candidates into Congress. It may even win the power to choose who shall run for president on both tickets, or at least to say who shall not run. The chances of doing this are best in the Democratic convention, where a third of the delegates can prevent nomination.

But if it wins only half success in the primaries, that is, can nominate men who are satisfactory only on one ticket and not on both tickets, either for Congress or the presidency, further success will be more doubtful. To win under these circumstances it would have to induce a vast number of men and women to break their old party ties, which would be one of the greatest feats in political history. It probably could

246

win a close election; it could hardly do so if the issues or the candidates got any great grip on the public. Still—people are not "regular" so often as they used to be and a good many of the Kluxers are one-time Progressives, who have learned how to bolt.

These are the factors in a problem that is making gray hair for national leaders in both parties. They know that the alien groups have little party loyalty, and will swing en masse behind a plank attacking the Klan. They know that the Klansmen, especially in the South, have always been so party-bound that even an anti-Klan plank could hardly make them change, but they can not be quite sure that the Klan influence might not do it this time. They can not guess, either, how many Klansmen might be led across the party line by a pro-Klan plank that would drive off all the aliens. The problem is to decide whether pro-Klan, anti-Klan or silence will be most profitable. The problem, it will be seen, is not the same for the two parties, because the bulk of the alien vote is now normally Democratic.

One more point should be noted. Although the Klan question will be uppermost in the minds of local politicians in over half the country, and will have a vital and perhaps deciding effect on the whole situation, it will be kept in the background as far as possible. Neither the Klan leaders, nor the politicians who are either with them or against them or on the fence, want it brought into the open. It will inevitably break out in spots, but on the whole we face an election in which one of the most important and decisive factors will be almost invisible and inaudible.

And if the Klan wins? That will mean in the first place the enactment of its national programme; restriction of immigration and naturalization, vigorous encouragement and some reform of the public schools, perhaps some economy and "good government" gestures, and the barring from office of Jews, Catholics and alien born. On other things the Klan will have no hold on officials or legislatures, and must let the winning party's programme take its course.

The Klan leaders might, of course, develop delusions of grandeur, run wild, meddle with many things and even try to persecute some one. But they will not do this in their present temper, and they are very unlikely to change. Against excesses, stands in the first place the saving sense of fairness which in crises has held America back time and again. There is also the well-known fact that responsibility usually makes leaders more sober, rather than more reckless. And there is the final fact, already explained, that if Klan leaders do try to involve the Order in new issues, it will go to pieces.

They will be pressed to "broaden out" by the fanatics and grafters inside the Klan, and by advisers outside, who will lay before them many and plausible schemes. Some such efforts are already making trouble inside the Klan. The leaders will lose a number of

248

their followers with each refusal to support some folly, though less than if they adopted it. They will also begin to lose as soon as they have put through their programme, since the Klan is a limited reform movement, and as Horace Greeley said of the Know-nothings—"It would seem as devoid of the elements of persistence as an anti-cholera or anti-potato-rot party." So there is a very strong probability that the Klan, which almost requires a victory to live after election, will find that victory is just as sure a road to destruction, if a little slower.

The result in local elections will be about the same as heretofore. The Klan record so far shows that these victories will mostly be with reform tickets; most of the successes it has won have resulted in better local governments. But such victories, as the United States has dearly learned, are also short lived, however useful. There will be vigorous clean-ups, some economies, some ousting of non-Klan people from power, and then a restful pause. There are many signs that this is already happening in places where the Klan strength developed earliest.

So, either nationally or locally, the fall election would seem to be the beginning of the end of the Klan on its present basis, whether it wins or loses. The leaders expect to make the organization permanent, after its immediate issues have passed, through its educational and good citizenship programme and some vague plans for governmental reforms. This might be done, but the programme, so far, is so nebulous that it presents no basis for forming any conclusions. It would make of the Klan a very different organization.

It appears, then, that the Klan is a great and growing power in politics, a power whose sudden rise is one of the most amazing in history—almost incredible. Its methods in this field are even more effective than in other fields, but—largely because they are not unusual—are less open to criticism leveled exclusively at the Klan. Their methods are unusual in that they have been raised to an uncanny efficiency.

The Klan's aims, in local campaigns, must usually command approval, and are supported nationally by a very large body of opinion which at the same time condemns the Klan organization and methods, and its standard of narrow and exclusive Americanism. It is sharply restricted to its own limited field by nature of its membership, is hardly likely to go outside it, and faces sure and swift destruction when, or if, it does. Its success will be great unless the elements it attacks contrive an opposition both solid and clever, and its success be measured almost exactly by the ability the opposition shows. Its chance of success, finally, is considerable, but the victory will have within itself factors likely to lead to disorganization.

If I may go back for a brief review of the previous chapters, it would seem that the evidence shows that the Klan is to-day a great power for good or evil in every phase of life, as well as in politics. It has made a tremendous recent growth, following important reforms, and can no longer be considered a gang of hoodlums and criminals, or simply a mob. Instead it is respectable, largely composed of very decent, well meaning and well behaved people of the kind who are the backbone of the nation. Its "lunatic fringe" and parasitic elements are large and dangerous, but not typical nor remarkable.

It has sprung up because of very real grievances and evils, in response for a growing demand for reform which was seeking leadership. It offers this leadership, brings the movement to a high intensity, unity and fine morale. It presents solutions which—whether right or wrong—appeal in many ways to certain types of minds, and it has grown so amazingly, largely because there is to-day, as far as these problems and this demand for reform go, no alternative except to join the Klan or be content with conversation. It has done much good, both in improving the conduct of its members, in influencing the conduct of others and in cleaning up bad local conditions.

But when all this has been granted, the fact remains that the Klan also involves and intensifies great evils. Its use of violence has been so largely controlled that it is now inconsiderable. Its nomenclature and regalia are after all more ridiculous than dangerous. Its acceptance of so many worthless members may—perhaps—be excused in a new and fast growing organization. But the terroristic symbolism remains, and an actual use of terrorism persists, even though it be only through scientific application of that "social and economic pressure" which is customary in any exercise of public opinion. The meddling with private affairs is abominable, in spite of some good that results. It is a sure road to greater evils, and is indefensible in principle, intolerable in any free society. This the Klan is trying to eliminate, to be sure, but it is a great and actual evil.

If it does cure these things, however, there remains and will remain until the very nature of the Klan itself changes, its fundamental principles of secrecy, espionage, and native, white, Protestant supremacy. These things are inconsistent with Americanism under a Declaration which holds that all men are created free and equal; they are dangerous, destructive, creative of disunity and hatred and so long as they exist will make impossible a free and united nation. They can not be too strongly condemned.

Yet—I have been unable to frame any indictment of the Klan for these sins which does not cover other secret organizations, based also on narrow race and religious division. No reason has appeared why it must be suppressed so long as they are tolerated. The Klan can claim that these other bodies threaten Americanism directly as well as indirectly, while its own menace is only indirect and its direct action is defensive of the national spirit. It can claim also that these other secret organizations were first in the field, chose the weapons and gave the provocation, and that it has no choice but to fight them on their own ground. If that is true the blame for the situation rests on them, not on the Klan. It may not be true, but it has not been disproved.

From these facts it may be argued that the Klan, in spite of all its evils and dangers, may be good for the country, like a noxious medicine, may clear the atmosphere, like a thunder-storm. Certainly there is need of a better national digestion and of a clearer fresher air. It is, I suppose, a matter of personal choice whether one prefers to endure the illness a little longer or until it grows worse, or to take a violent and disruptive dose, which may prove poisonous.

I should like in conclusion to make a few general observations about the Klan which do not rest on definite proof and which may be no more than personal opinion, though I believe them of greater importance than that.

The first is, that the Klan is no hideous menace. It can do much harm, beyond doubt, and will do some. The prejudices it has released, the turmoil it has aroused, its wrong principles and wrong methods are all dangerous and might be serious indeed. Perhaps I am a little weary of many menaces, but in spite of these things I can not see that it is likely to do any very great or irreparable harm.

For one thing, we can depend largely on the general

good sense and fairness of the members. They are not a mob; not naturally cruel or unjust. The flare of prejudice will die quickly, unless fed from the outside. One correspondent declares that if the Klan is not suppressed it will be burning convents in New York, as was done by a mob in the 'thirties. If this is possible, then the decidedly alien government of New York needs overhauling, even as the Klan says. But I can not believe it possible, even with all allowances made for what the mob spirit may do with ordinarily decent folk. And the Klan leaders whom I have seen would be the first to stop such an attempted outrage, should the city government fail in its duty.

In the second place the Klan is getting better. Some of its worst features are almost gone, others are going. The leaders are of a more balanced type than at first, are being sobered by power, and the better class membership that has recently joined, is taking control.

As to "invisible government" that seems any unusual kind of sheer nonsense. The Klan is a reform movement, working largely through politics, using pretty much the usual political methods. Any group control of government is a menace, but we have survived a good many of them, some of which were invisible, and the Klan is not the worst of the lot. Our system provides the means by which any group can be ousted if it gets too strong or overbearing; the Klan itself is proof of this, since it is a reaction against other groups which have had much power and used it unwisely. Its political programme may be wrong, but it is at worst, negative. If it does stop immigration, for example, and we need more aliens, the lack can very easily be righted.

Besides all this, the Klan can hardly live long in anything much like its present form. It is a protest movement, a reform drive, and as such is almost certain to be killed by either success or failure. It has, indeed, within itself the elements of sure decay, grounds for dissension, for jealousies, for division. Moreover it is too high pitched; no body of men can long hold the camp-meeting fervor which the Klan now boasts without complete reaction. It may be changed in ways which will give it longer life, but that is a possibility outside the scope of this report.

It seems clear, also, that the Klan is doing much good along with the harm. Its local reforms are likely to be as temporary as the fervor and prejudices it has aroused, but they can at least be set off against those evils. And its services in stirring up thought and focussing attention on the evils which now threaten Americanism are very great. This might lead to solutions, even if the Klan does not find them or bring them itself.

For all these reasons it again seems clear that the Klan, in spite of its obvious evils and dangers, is far less likely to destroy the nation or to do it serious injury, than are several other of our present menaces.

THE CHALLENGE OF THE KLAN

It could not begin to do the damage, for example, that is possible from a real coalition of alien elements which would be almost as likely as in the Klan to win control of the government; it is far less dangerous than is the state of mind which permits some of the country's most trusted officers to use their places as stepping stones to jobs where their political friendships can be cashed in at a high figure; less dangerous than the far more common attitude that in politics the standard of conduct is neither justice, fairness nor public service but what can be "got away with"; less dangerous even than our usual custom of judging public men and giving them our support with regard not at all to their ability or value to the country as a whole, but solely for their willingness to scratch our own personal backs and their success in doing it. Since we have been able to survive all these other menaces, we can probably recover from the Klan!

The most serious menace in the Klan movement is quite different from any of those usually shrieked about. It is that the Klan may prevent reforms which are bitterly needed. There is an urgent demand for some drastic action to stop the flood of unassimilable immigration, to Americanize or restrict the powers of the alien groups which are deliberately hostile to Americanism, to meet and defeat the influences which are trying to pervert and degrade American thought and purpose. The danger is that the Klan, by using the wrong methods in attacking these problems and failing to solve them, may discredit all other efforts, and open the way for a period of un-American domination that will wreck forever our national purposes and opportunities.

I have been asked by several people whether there is behind the Klan some mighty Machiavellian brain, controlling the movement and directing it to hidden and possibly Satanic ends. I have seen no sign of such a force. The leaders with whom I have talked speak as those having authority in themselves, and there is certainly no Machiavellian brain among them. On the other hand, they are apparently overwhelmed with their own success, vastly sobered by it, troubled as to what to do with it, fearful of leadership, but driven on by the forces they have raised.

Finally it would seem practically impossible to destroy the Klan forthwith. The momentum is too great, the demand for some action of the kind it promises, too intense. The leaders are leading only in the sense that they are out in front; they, as well as the rank and file, are in the grip of their own ideas and can not stop. The Klan, as I have said, has grown from a few thousand to a few millions in the face of ridicule, prosecution, persecution and weakness. Now it is rich, powerful and feared—I can conceive of nothing likely to be effective against it until it begins to break down from the inside. The only possibility is to find other and better means of meeting the problems and evils which gave it strength, and this method the most bitter of its enemies are the least inclined to follow.

The movement can, however, be guided, its dangers lessened, its really valuable possibilities put to better use. The leaders themselves seem almost pitifully anxious for guidance, they are seeking it everywhere and employing the best minds they can get in the hope of learning what to do—what they can do—with their power. They are suspicious, also, having had much experience with all kinds of bad advice. But counsel which they believe to be disinterested, patriotic and fair, they will welcome.

It is to this, it seems to me, that those who fear the Klan movement should now turn their energies, though there is undoubted danger for them in such an effort, for the opprobrium which followed the Know-nothings may very easily attach to any one who gives aid or comfort to the Klan. But there is nothing else in sight that promises to have any value whatever in dealing with the movement.

THE END

APPENDIX

The Constitution of the Ku Klux Klan

(The first four sections of the Constitution will be found in
Chapter III)

EMPEROR OF THE INVISIBLE EMPIRE, HIS DUTIES AND PRIVILEGES.

Article V.

Section 1. The Emperor of the Invisible Empire shall have
entire charge of Kloranic, Ritualistic and Philosophic work of
this Order, and he shall be an ex-officio member of all Imperial,
Grand, Great and Klan bodies. His term of office shall be for
life.

Section 2. In the event of a vacancy in his office, his successor
shall be called and installed by the Grand Dragons of the various
Realms, in the same manner as set forth in Article IX of this
constitution.

Section 3. He shall create and cause to be promulgated all
countersigns, passwords, ritualistic or kloranic work and secret
signs, symbols and work of this Order. He shall design, or
cause to be designed, all paraphernalia, regalia, uniforms, costumes, emblems, insignia, flags, banners, and jewelry for individual wear, honorary and official jewels, books, pamphlets and
literature of this Order. All costumes, designs, symbols or other
insignia officially adopted by this Order, whether created by him
or not, shall be recognized as official, and shall be received by
the members of this Order.

259

THE CHALLENGE OF THE KLAN

Section 4. He shall have the sole power to create all titles and honors within this Order on whomsoever he may elect, and shall issue and sign all certificates or diplomas relative thereto, and cause to be affixed thereon the great Imperial Seal of the Order.

THE IMPERIAL KLONVOKATION.

ARTICLE VI.

Section 1. The Imperial Klonvokation shall be the sole legislative body of this Order; therefore, it shall have original jurisdiction in all matters pertaining to creating and amending this Constitution and Laws, the regulation, government and general welfare of this Order. It shall have power to enact laws for the regulation of its own procedure, for the government of the Invisible Empire, Realms, Provinces and Klans, and for the general control and management of the business of this Order, and to provide penalties for the violation thereof. It shall have power to prescribe the rights, privileges, duties, and responsibilities of Realms, Provinces and Klans, and of all officers and members of this Order, and finally to determine the same. The Imperial Klonvokation shall meet bienially in the month of September on day and at place to be fixed by the Imperial Wizard.

Section 2. The Imperial Klonvokation shall be composed of all Imperial Officers, the Grand Dragons and an elected delegate (Klepeer) from each organized Realm; the Great Titan, and an elected delegate (Klepeer) from each Province. (Exalted Cyclops from Klans that are in good standing by reason of having paid all Imperial, Realm and Province taxes shall be entitled to one vote each therein, which can not be delegated, and which shall be deducted from the total vote of their Realm.) Each organized Realm (State) represented in the Klonvokation shall be entitled to one vote for each One Hundred or majority fraction thereof of Klansmen in good standing in that Realm at the end of the calendar quarter next preceding the meeting of the Imperial Klonvokation as shown by the records of the Imperial Palace. The total vote of each Realm, after deducting

APPENDIX

the vote of the Exalted Cyclops present, thus determined shall be equally divided among the representatives present at the Klonvokation. States not organized into Realms shall be entitled to one representative for each state who shall be elected by the Chartered Klans thereof and shall have same voting power as in Realms. Provided, however, that in no event shall the conditions of this section operate to increase the basis of representation for a State or Realm as herein provided in this section of Article VI of the Constitution and Laws. Courtesy cards may be issued entitling the holders of same to seat outside the boundaries of the regular Klepeers' seats, the holders of the courtesy privilege, however, having no voting privilege and must be members in good standing, in Klans in good standing in the Imperial, Realm and Province funds.

Section 3. The active officers of the Imperial Klonvokation in convention assembled shall be a president and a secretary. The Imperial Klaliff shall be its president and the Imperial Kligrapp shall be its secretary and recording officer. Other Imperial Officers may act as chairmen of Committees, or constitute committees. All acts of the Klonvokation shall become effective within one hour after their passage unless vetoed by the Imperial Wizard within that time, in which event the Klonvokation may pass the act over the veto of the Imperial Wizard by three-fourths (¾) vote of the said Klonvokation.

THE IMPERIAL KLONCILIUM.

Article VII.

Section 1. The Imperial Kloncilium shall be the supreme advisory board of this Order and shall be composed of all the Imperial Officers named in Article VIII.

Section 2. The Imperial Kloncilium shall be the Supreme Tribunal of Justice of this Order and shall have full appellate jurisdiction to hear and finally determine all appeals of whatever nature presented to it affecting the relationship and constitutional rights and privileges of Realms and Provinces, and Klans and members of his Order in unorganized states.

261

THE CHALLENGE OF THE KLAN

Section 3. It shall have full power and authority, acting in the presence of the Imperial Wizard or his authorized representative, to act in the interim between sessions of the Imperial Klonvokation.

Section 4. It shall meet in regular session in the month of July each year on call of the Imperial Wizard, but special sessions may be held at any other time on call of the Imperial Wizard when same is deemed necessary by him or when he is requested in writing to do so by five members thereof.

Section 5. Nine members present, in person or by proxy, of the Imperial Kloncilium, including the Imperial Wizard, or his authorized representative, shall constitute a quorum for the transaction of all matters coming before it, except where otherwise provided herein.

Section 6. Decisions of the Imperial Kloncilium on all matters of a judiciary nature coming before it for adjudication shall be final when same are ratified by the Imperial Wizard.

Section 7. Between the meetings of the Imperial Kloncilium, whenever, in the judgment of the Imperial Wizard, it shall become necessary for it to consider any matter or thing whatsoever, he may submit the matter to the members of the Imperial Kloncilium in writing by mail or otherwise, and their votes thereon shall be cast in writing by mail or otherwise within a time limit to be fixed by the Imperial Wizard.

Section 8. The Imperial Kligrapp shall be the Secretary and recording officer of the Imperial Kloncilium.

IMPERIAL OFFICERS.

ARTICLE VIII.

Section 1. Hereafter the Imperial officers of this Order shall be sixteen in number, and their official titles shall be as follows:
The Imperial Wizard (Supreme Chief Executive).
Imperial Klaliff (Supreme 1st Vice-Pres.).
Imperial Klazik (Supreme 2nd Vice-Pres.).
Imperial Klokard (Supreme Lecturer).
Imperial Kludd (Supreme Chaplain).

262

APPENDIX

Imperial Kligrapp (Supreme Secretary).
Imperial Klabee (Supreme Treasurer).
Imperial Kladd (Supreme Conductor).
Imperial Klarogo (Supreme Inner-Guard).
Imperial Klexter (Supreme Outer-Guard).
Imperial Klonsel (Supreme Attorney).
Imperial Night-Hawk (Supreme Courier)
and four Imperial Klokann (Constituting a Board of Auditors and supreme advisers).

These shall be known as the Imperial Wizard and his fifteen GENII.

IMPERIAL WIZARD.

ARTICLE IX.

Section 1. The Imperial Wizard is the supreme chief executive of this Order. He shall be elected by the Grand Dragons. To elect the Imperial Wizard, the Grand Dragons shall meet in executive session upon the call of the Imperial Kligrapp. Each Grand Dragon shall cast his vote the number of votes representing his Realm, in the Klonvokation as shown by the records of the Imperial Palace on the first day of the quarter, on which election is held; this vote to be ascertained in the same manner as set forth in Section V, Article 6. If no result is determined after three ballots all names must be dropped except the three receiving the highest number of votes; if no result is determined at the end of three more ballots, all names must be dropped except the two receiving the highest number of votes. No nomination shall be made. No motions except a motion to recess shall be entertained during said election. No adjournment shall be taken until after the completion of the election. Any Klansman in good standing in any Klan in good standing as determined by the records of the Imperial Palace is eligible to be chosen Imperial Wizard. While the Grand Dragons are in session for the purpose of electing an Imperial Wizard, they are prohibited from having any communication of any nature what-

THE CHALLENGE OF THE KLAN

soever with any one outside of their meeting from the time they are called to order until they have finally elected an Imperial Wizard.

Section 2. The Imperial Wizard shall hold office for a period of four years or until his successor is elected and installed. He shall be removed for just cause by the Imperial Kloncilium after charges have been preferred and a trial held, upon a three-fourths vote of said body, in session assembled, subject to the approval of the Grand Dragons who shall be immediately convened in executive session by the Imperial Kligrapp.

Section 3. Upon the death or removal of the Imperial Wizard from office, the Imperial Klaliff shall immediately succeed to that office and shall govern until a successor to the Imperial Wizard is installed. In the event the Imperial Wizard is removed from office, a successor shall be named at the earliest possible date thereafter, consistent with careful judgment in the selection.

DUTIES, PREROGATIVES AND POWERS OF THE IMPERIAL WIZARD.

ARTICLE X.

Section 1. Being the Supreme Chief Executive of this Order, the Imperial Wizard shall have and hold supreme authority and power within this Constitution in all administrative matters, and to act in any and all matters not prescribed in this Constitution, when in his judgment the best interest of this Order warrants. He may delegate such authority to his subordinate executive or administrative officers as he may deem necessary, but the Imperial Authority of this Order shall ever center and be vested in him and shall not be divided.

Section 2. He shall specify the duties of all officers regardless of rank or station, of whatever department, bureau, or division, other than those duties enumerated in this Constitution, and shall require such duties to be properly performed on penalty of removal from office.

264

APPENDIX

Section 3. He shall issue charters for Klans, specify conditions on which charters shall be issued, and shall have the power to open and close charters of Klans in his discretion or upon request of a Klan. He shall have full and unchallengable authority and power to suspend or revoke charters of Klans, for cause.

Section 4. He shall promulgate all countersigns and passwords, and any and all other secret signs and work of this Order, created by the Emperor.

Section 5. He shall have supreme supervision over all departments of this Order.

Section 6. He shall have full authority to issue decrees, edicts, mandates, rulings and instructions covering any matter not specifically set forth in this Constitution, or emphasizing any matter of this Constitution, and all such decrees, edicts, mandates, rulings and instructions must be respected and obeyed promptly and faithfully by all members of this Order on penalty of banishment.

Section 7. He shall manufacture, or cause to be manufactured, all paraphernalia, regalia, uniforms, costumes, emblems, insignia, flags, banners, jewelry for individual wear, jewels for official use, clerical forms, books, pamphlets, literature, advertising matter, stationery, etc., etc., and no other design, emblem, insignia or form or thing, article or articles shall be recognized, countenanced or used by this Order or any member of same. All designs, emblems or other insignia officially adopted by the Emperor whether created by him or not, shall be recognized as official and duly respected by all members of this Order.

Section 8. He shall request of the Imperial Klonvokation such legislation as he deems wise for the best interest of this Order in its government, regulation and promulgation.

Section 9. He shall have full power and authority to remove from office at any time any officer of this Order, other than an Imperial Officer, of any rank or station or capacity, or any employee whomsoever, on the ground of incompetency, disloyalty, neglect of duty, or for unbecoming conduct.

Section 10. He shall have full authority and power to appoint all Imperial Officers and Grand Dragons, and their terms of

THE CHALLENGE OF THE KLAN

office shall be designated by him unless otherwise provided for herein.

Section 11. He shall have and hold full and original authority and power, office and title of "Supreme Kleagle," and is fully authorized and empowered to solicit applicants for membership in this Order, to collect and receipt for Klectokons, and admit to membership, in this Order, any person or any number of persons at any time and in any place he may choose, provided such person or persons qualify under the requirements of Article IV, Section 1, of this Constitution.

Section 12. He shall issue and sign all commissions or other credentials of this order in promulgating same, and affix the Imperial Seal thereto; and he shall contract in the name of this Order, with other members for its extension, financing, management, operation and business interests, and shall fix the compensation therefor.

Section 13. Whenever a question of paramount importance to the interest, well-being or prosperity of this Order arises, not provided for in this Constitution, he shall have full power and authority to determine such question, and his decision, which he shall report to the Imperial Klonvokation if requested, shall be final.

DUTIES OF IMPERIAL OFFICERS.

ARTICLE XI.

Section 1. IMPERIAL KLALIFF: Is the second highest officer of this Order; he shall be the president of the Imperial Klonvokation, and perform such other duties as may be required by the Imperial Wizard.

Section 2. IMPERIAL KLAZIK: Is the second vice-president of this Order, and he shall be the executive head of the department of Realms, and shall perform such other duties as may be required by the Imperial Wizard.

Section 3. IMPERIAL KLOKARD: The duties of the Imperial Klokard shall be to disseminate Klankraft, and perform such duties as may be required by the Imperial Wizard.

266

APPENDIX

Section 4. IMPERIAL KLUDD: Is the Chaplain of the Imperial Klonvokation and shall perform such other duties as may be required by the Imperial Wizard.

Section 5. IMPERIAL KLIGRAPP: Is the Supreme Secretary and recording officer of this Order. He shall be in charge of secretarial work and shall be the custodian of the Imperial records and the Imperial Seal. He shall receive and receipt for all funds coming from any source whatsoever. He shall transmit all such funds in his possession to the Imperial Klabee (Supreme Treasurer) at the close of each day, taking his receipt therefor. He shall be the secretary of the Imperial Klonvokation and shall act as secretary of the Imperial Kloncilium and shall have general supervision of all the clerical work and workings. He shall keep an accurate account of the receipts and disbursements. He shall sign all papers, vouchers and other documents requiring his signature or attestation. He shall prepare and submit a report of the workings of his office to each session of the Imperial Klonvokation. He shall furnish the Imperial Kloncilium when requested with such information as they desire with reference to his office. He shall give bond for the faithful and honest performance of the duties of his office in some reliable bonding or surety company in the sum of $25,000.00, the said bond to be approved by the Imperial Kloncilium. He shall not assume the duties of his office until all these requirements are complied with.

Section 6. IMPERIAL KLABEE: Is the Supreme Treasurer of this Order and is, therefore, the custodian of its funds. It shall be his duty to demand of the Imperial Kligrapp at the close of each day all funds received by the Imperial Kligrapp and he shall receipt the Imperial Kligrapp therefor, and make a deposit of funds once each day in some bank or banks, designated by the Imperial Kloncilium. These funds shall be carried in the name of the Knights of the Ku Klux Klan and shall be paid out only upon the signature of the Imperial Klabee, countersigned by the Imperial Wizard. He shall keep an accurate record of all receipts and disbursements made by him, and shall make a full and complete report of the receipts and disbursements of his office to the Imperial Kloncilium at its regular

267

annual meeting, and to the Imperial Klonvokation at its regular meeting. He shall perform such other duties as may be required of him by the Imperial Wizard. For the faithful and honest performance of his duties he shall give bond in some bonding or surety company to be approved by the Imperial Kloncilium in a sum not less than $50,000.00. The amount of this bond may be increased at any time by the Imperial Kloncilium.

Section 7. IMPERIAL KLADD: Shall perform such duties as may be required of him by the Imperial Wizard.

Section 8. IMPERIAL KLAROGO: Is inner guard at all Imperial Kloncilium and Imperial Klonvokation meetings and shall perform such other duties as may be required by the Imperial Wizard.

Section 9. IMPERIAL KLEXTER: Is outer guard at all meetings of the Imperial Kloncilium and Imperial Klonvokation, and shall perform such other duties as may be required by the Imperial Wizard.

Section 10. IMPERIAL KLONSEL: Is Supreme Attorney or legal adviser of this Order and shall perform such other duties as may be required by the Imperial Wizard.

Section 11. IMPERIAL NIGHT-HAWK: Is the head of the Department of Investigation, and shall perform such other duties as may be required by the Imperial Wizard.

Section 12. THE IMPERIAL KLOKANN: Is the Supreme Board of Auditors and Special Advisers. It shall be composed of four members, each of whom shall bear the official title of "Imperial Klokan." The chairman of this board shall be known as "Chief Imperial Klokan." The duties of this Board shall be to audit the books, records and reports of the Imperia Kligrapp and the Imperial Klabee and the clerical records of this Order, and to make a written report at each regular session of the Imperial Klonvokation and the Imperial Kloncilium. It shall recommend to the Imperial Wizard such plans and methods as it deems wise for the welfare of this Order, and it shall perform such other duties as may be required of it, and each member thereof, individually, shall perform such other duties as may be required of him by the Imperial Wizard.

APPENDIX

KLEAGLES AND GIANTS.

ARTICLE XII.

Section 1. A Kleagle is an organizer or field worker of this Order, and shall be appointed only by or under the direct or delegated authority of the Imperial Wizard, and shall work by and under his requirements and instructions.

Section 2. The Imperial Wizard, being by virtue of his office the Supreme Kleagle, shall have full power and authority to commission and appoint members of this Order as Kleagles, and he shall have full power to remove from office any Kleagle of any rank, grade or station whatsoever.

Section 3. All authority, power, privileges and prerogatives that may be vested in, or conferred upon the office of Kleagle of any rank below the Supreme Kleagle shall be derived from the Supreme Kleagle and delegated by him only, and same must be evidenced by a documentary commission setting forth such authority and power so delegated.

Section 4. Kleagles of whatever rank below the Supreme Kleagle shall be employed under contract stipulations, and they shall give bond in some reliable bonding or surety company in such amount as may be required by the Imperial Wizard.

Section 5. Kleagles of whatever rank, grade, or station, must thoroughly familiarize themselves with the Kloran, laws, principles, objects, history, usages and mannerisms of this Order, and must be able to demonstrate same in an intelligent and proficient manner.

Section 6. The title of Giant may apply by gradation to all officers who have served one or more terms as the chief executive officer of the Invisible Empire and of subordinate jurisdictions thereof. A Klan Giant is one who has served as Exalted Cyclops; a Great Giant is one who has served as Great Titan; a Grand Giant is one who has served as Grand Dragon; an Imperial Giant is one who has served as Imperial Wizard. The title is not conferred on an officer until his successor has been duly installed. The title Giant shall in all cases be conferred

269

upon the recommendation of the next officer above in rank. This honorary title shall be conferred in recognition of regular and faithful services performed as prescribed by the Constitution and Laws of this Order. The Grand Dragon of a Realm shall, at all times, keep in his office a list of the Giants in that Realm and shall, whenever possible, use such Giants for special service.

PARAPHERNALIA, REGALIA, EMBLEMS, ENSIGNS, INSIGNIA, ETC.

Article XIII.

Section 1. All ensigns, standards, flags or banners, and all emblems, insignia, paraphernalia, regalia, uniforms, and costumes, and all designs thereof of our original society—the Ku Klux Klan—are retained and officially re-adopted as property of this Order under its now incorporate name of Knights of the Ku Klux Klan.

Section 2. All designs, ensigns, flags, standards, banners, emblems, insignia, seals, paraphernalia, regalia, uniforms, costumes, etc., and all clerical forms or matters to be printed, shall be adopted by or designed by or under the directions of the Emperor only.

Section 3. All articles, designs and things referred to or implied in Sections 1 and 2, above, and Article X, Section 10, of this Constitution, and all property, real and personal, shall ever be and remain the property of this Order and such supplies can only be procured from the Imperial Wizard by the required requisition therefor, and this also shall apply to all supplies used by any subordinate jurisdiction, and any and all jewelry or other articles used by a member.

Section 4. Any article or thing, regardless of form, or of what material it shall be made, or for what purpose it shall be made, or to what use it shall be subjected, if it bears an emblem or an insignia of this Order, shall belong to and is the property of this Order; and such article or thing can not legally bear an emblem, insignia, or design of this Order without written authority of the Imperial Wizard, and can only be procured

270

APPENDIX

through him, and can be used only by a member or by such person or persons properly coming under the protection of this Order by authority of the Imperial Wizard. If such article or thing or other property be intrusted to or permitted to be in the possession of a member, or other person, as set forth above, it must be surrendered on official demand by an Exalted Cyclops or the Imperial Wizard. If a member has in his possession any article or property of this Order, and voluntarily discontinues his membership, or is banished from membership, or in any other manner his connection with this Order is severed, such article or articles, thing or things, must be immediately returned or surrendered by him to an Exalted Cyclops, Great Titan, Grand Dragon, or to the Imperial Wizard, and he shall be given a receipt for same. Upon his failure to do so within thirty days the Exalted Cyclops or other officer shall take action necessary to regain the actual possession of such article or articles. All rights, privileges and use of all such designs, emblems, insignia, etc., cited or implied above, are strictly reserved by this Order.

Section 5. It shall be unlawful for any person or persons, company, firm or corporation, to manufacture or cause to be manufactured, catalog or cause to be cataloged, advertise or cause to be advertised, sell or offer for sale or cause same to be done, any article or design whatsoever of this Order or anything used by or properly belonging to this Order, unless such person or persons, company, firm or corporation, be duly licensed by the Imperial Wizard to manufacture, advertise or sell such article, designs or things, and even then, only by a strict adherence to the conditions, restrictions and directions specified in said license.

Section 6. It shall be unlawful for any member of this Order to purchase, cause to be purchased, or otherwise come into possession of any article or property of this Order from any person, company, firm or corporation, without authority to do so from the Imperial Wizard; he can procure such article from the Imperial Wizard only by making requisition therefor, and remitting the amount of money required. It shall be unlawful for any subordinate jurisdiction to procure any article or property of this Order, or any supplies, etc., used by it from any other source than the Imperial Wizard, or by his authority.

THE CHALLENGE OF THE KLAN

Section 7. If an unauthorized person shall have in his possession any article, or property of this Order, and this fact shall become known to a member, it shall be the sworn duty of such member to regain for this Order the actual possession of such article without delay; his failure to do so will jeopardize his membership.

COSTUMES, SEALS, ENSIGNS, SYMBOLS, ETC.

Article XIV.

Section 1. KLAN PARAPHERNALIA: Shall consist of altar furnishings as per Kloran, and such account books, forms, and other things as are necessary.

Section 2. COSTUMES: The official costume of this Order, shall be a white robe of light weight cotton cloth, made with cape of same material, and of proper length, with white girdle around waist, and insignia of this Order worn on the left breast. The cowl or helmet shall be made of same material as the robe, and with whatever material necessary to give it the proper stiffness, and so made that it will be collapsible, and when worn shall be of a cone shape. There shall be one red tassel attached to the peak of same. There shall be an apron of same material in both the front and rear, so as to completely conceal the identity of the wearer. The front apron shall have two holes of the proper size and location to facilitate the vision of the wearer. This shall be known as the Klansman's robe or costume. Costumes to be worn by active officers, of whatever rank or station, shall be of such design, and made of such material, and with the use of such colors, as may be prescribed by the Emperor.

Section 3. EMBLEMS AND SYMBOLS: Shall be such as may be designed or authorized by the Emperor.

Section 4. ENSIGNS, FLAGS AND STANDARDS: The official ensigns, flags and standards of this Order, together with all official banners, shall be of such shape, size and design as may be authorized by the Emperor.

272

THE CHALLENGE OF THE KLAN

Section 5. THE GRAND ENSIGN: The "Grand Ensign" or Banner of this Order shall be in the form of an isosceles triangle, five feet long and three feet wide at the staff. The material shall be yellow, with a red scalloped border about three inches in width. There shall be painted upon it in black, A Dracovolans, or Flying Dragon, with the following motto inscribed on it: "Quod Semper, quod ubique, quod ab omnibus." The tongue shall be painted in red with an arrow head end. The tail shall also end with an arrow head.

Section 6. SEAL: There shall be a Seal of this Order, which shall be known as the Great Imperial Seal. It shall bear the words, "Imperial Seal—Knights of the Ku Klux Klan," and shall be of such design as the Emperor shall direct. Each chartered Klan of this Order shall have a Seal bearing the name, number, and Realm of the Klan, together with the name of this Order, "Knights of the Ku Klux Klan," and shall be of such design as directed by the Emperor. This Seal must be procured by the Klan immediately after it shall have been chartered. Seals to be used by the various subordinate jurisdictions shall bear the name—"Knights of the Ku Klux Klan," and be of such design as the Emperor may direct.

Section 7. KLIKON AND SYMBOLS: The Klikon is the Sacred Picture of this Order, and as such must be rigidly safeguarded by whatever Klan or Klansman to whom it may be intrusted. The various symbols of this Order, used in its several Kloranic Orders, shall be such as are designed and authorized by the Emperor.

REVENUES AND PROPERTY TITLES.

ARTICLE XV.

Section 1. The revenues of this Order shall consist of: First, a percentage of each and every klectokon, whether paid to a Klan or to a Kleagle; such percentage to be determined by the Imperial Wizard. Second, a per capita tax, which shall be known as the Imperial Tax; which shall be a sum of money not to exceed fifteen (15c) cents per capita per month. Third,

THE CHALLENGE OF THE KLAN

all profits realized from the placing of paraphernalia, regalia, supplies, jewelry, uniforms, costumes, stationery, and any and all other articles used in the work of this Order, or by any member. Fourth, all interest accruing on investments made by this Order.

Section 2. The Imperial Tax shall begin with the month immediately succeeding the month in which a Klan is chartered, and is due and payable on the first day of each calendar quarter thereafter; the Kligrapp of each Klan shall remit the same with his regular quarterly report—his failure to do so will subject the charter of that Klan to suspension or cancellation. The Imperial Tax is hereby levied upon each and every Klan now chartered and which may be hereafter chartered, and the Imperial Wizard has full authority and power to collect same.

Section 3. The revenues of a Realm shall consist of: First, such portion of the Imperial revenue received from that Realm as may be fixed by proclamation of the Imperial Wizard. Second, a per capita tax, to be known as a Province Tax, in such amount as the Klonverse of each Province may determine, in no case to be less than 8⅓ cents per month.

REALMS.

ARTICLE XVI.

Section 1. A Realm may be organized within a state or states of the United States, or other territorial sub-division when recommended by a committee of three Realm Officers from other States appointed by the Imperial Klazik for that purpose.

Section 2. A Realm is organized on the declaration of the Imperial Wizard, and with such declaration he shall appoint and name all officers thereof and shall furnish laws and regulations for the government of that Realm, and such appointment of officers and such laws, if not in conflict with this Constitution, shall be effective until the convention of the initial Klorero of that Realm after its organization; at which time the Klorero will proceed to elect all of its elective officers, and adopt laws for

274

the government of that Realm, but such laws adopted and such elections held shall not be inconsistent with this Constitution and the laws of this Order. Such laws and amendments of laws adopted at this time or at any future Klorero must be ratified by the Grand Dragon and the Imperial Wizard before the same becomes effective as law.

Section 3. The Klorero of a Realm shall be composed of all Grand Officers of that Realm, Great Titans and Great Officers of provinces within that Realm, and five Klepeers from each Province in said Realm. Grand Officers, Great Titans and Great Officers shall be entitled to one vote each. The five Klepeers shall be entitled to one vote for each one hundred Klansmen or major fraction thereof in good standing within the province that they represent, said Klepeers present to divide this vote equally. Exalted Cyclops shall have the same voting rights, and under the same conditions as in the Klonvokation.

Section 4. The Klorero shall possess no power to interfere with the Imperial Wizard in his plans and purposes in the promulgation of this Order within its respective bounds.

Section 5. The Klorero shall provide its own revenue to meet the expenses of its convention and clerical obligations.

Section 6. The officers of a Realm shall be a Grand Dragon, who shall be President of the Klorero; he shall be appointed by the Imperial Wizard for a term of office designated in his appointment or during faithful service and good behavior, and shall govern his Realm in a manner not inconsistent with this Constitution, or the instructions and directions of the Imperial Klazik; Grand Klaliff, second highest officer of a Realm, who shall be vice-president of the Klorero; Grand Klokard, lecturer; Grand Kludd, chaplain; Grand Kligrapp, secretary; Grand Klabee, treasurer; Grand Kladd, conductor; Grand Klarogo, inner guard; Grand Klexter, outer guard; and a Grand Night-Hawk. These shall be known as the Grand Dragon and his nine Hydras. Officers of a Realm, other than the Grand Dragon, shall be elected by the Klorero on the nomination of the Grand Dragon, and such election must be ratified by the Imperial Klazik prior to their installation.

Section 7. The Grand Dragon and Great Titans of each Realm

275

shall be required to meet *en banc* on the third Monday of July of each year. The first meeting to be held on the third Monday of July, 1923, at a place designated by the Imperial Klazik. The object of the meeting is to discuss Klan problems and to suggest solutions therefor.

PROVINCES.

Article XVII.

Section 1. The Grand Dragon shall designate the bounds of a Province in his Realm, and shall form new Provinces as the development warrants, but in number not to exceed six Provinces in any one Realm, except by permission of the Imperial Wizard. Desiring to form a Province he shall procure permission from the Imperial Klazik. Upon receipt of such permission he shall notify all Klans to be incorporated in that Province, naming the officers appointed by him, and formally declaring such Province formed, and report immediately such formation to the Imperial Klazik.

Section 2. At the initial convention of a Klonverse of a Province, the elective officers of that Province shall be elected, but such election must be ratified by the Grand Dragon of that Realm, and such officers elected and ratified shall be installed by the Grand Dragon or by his duly appointed deputy, and they shall govern the Province under the direction and instructions of the Grand Dragon.

Section 3. A Klonverse shall be composed of all the Grand Officers of the Realm; all Great Officers of that Province and four Klepeers from each Klan in good standing in that Province. The Grand Officers and Great Officers shall each be entitled to one vote. The Klepeers shall be entitled to one vote for each one hundred Klansmen or major fraction thereof in good standing in their Klan and they shall divide the vote of their Klan equally.

Section 4. The officers of a Province shall hereafter be: A Great Titan, the highest officer of a Province, and President of

276

the Klonverse; three great Klaliffs, who shall compose an Advisory Board; a Great Kligrapp, secretary; a Great Klabee, treasurer; a Great Kludd, chaplain; and a Great Night-Hawk. These officers shall be known as the Great Titan and his Seven Furies, and their terms of office shall be from the date of their installation until the next convention of the Klonverse, or until their successors shall have been elected and installed.

Section 5. The Great Titan of a Province shall be appointed by the Grand Dragon of the Realm, with the consent and approval of the Imperial Klazik, but all other officers of a Province shall be elected by the Klonverse on the nomination of the Great Titan.

Section 6. The function of the Klonverse is social and fraternal, for the purpose of promoting good fellowship within the bounds of that Province, and stimulating and developing interest in this Order, and its mission and work.

Section 7. The Klonverse shall meet in regular session each calendar year, at such place as it may select, and at such time as the Great Titan may designate—provided the Klonverse must hold its session at least thirty days prior to the convention of the Klorero of that Realm.

KLANS.

ARTICLE XVIII.

Section 1-a. In States having a perfected Realm organization, the Grand Dragon shall designate the location of new Klans to be instituted, and shall stipulate the number of charter petitioners necessary to institute a new Klan.

Section 1-b. In States having no Realm organization, the King Kleagle shall be the judge of the location and number of petitioners necessary to institute a new Klan.

Section 2. The Kleagle in charge of the organization of a Klan shall remain in charge and be responsible until that Klan is duly chartered and its officers elected and installed.

Section 3-a. Upon the organization of a Klan, a vote shall be had on the petitioners, and if there be three negative votes cast on the ballot as a whole, then an individual ballot shall be had by balloting on the petitioners one at a time, three negative ballots rejecting. After a Klan has been organized and prior to the issuance and closing of its charter, charter applicants must be submitted to the Klan in klonklave assembled; if any Klansman present knows any just reason that disqualifies an applicant for membership, he must rise to his feet and challenge that applicant and state his reasons for so doing; this done, the Provisional Exalted Cyclops, or the Kleagle in charge acting as such, shall refer the application to the Klokann and the Klokann shall investigate the application on the basis of the grounds of objection, and they shall report on such applicant at the next subsequent klonklave, if possible, or at the very earliest possible date thereafter, at which klonklave final action shall be taken. An applicant who has been finally rejected can not apply again until after the expiration of twelve months from date of rejection. If after a careful investigation the Klokann finds that the objector was in error, they shall report accordingly and recommend the passage of the applicant, and the Klan shall take definite and final action on the report of the Klokann.

Section 3-b. Applications for membership in chartered Klans shall be read three times in Klonklave assembled, and opportunity given each member present to make objections. All objections may be made in writing, signed by the objector and delivered to the Klokann, whose duty it shall be to investigate the objections and make their findings and report the same to the Klan body for its adoption or rejection. All petitions must be made in writing on Form K-115.

Section 3-c. An applicant who has been finally rejected can not apply again until after the expiration of twelve months from date of rejection and shall be within the jurisdiction of that Klan for a period of three years. Provided, however, upon request of the Klokann of that Klan through regular channels the Grand Dragon of organized Realms or the Imperial Wizard in unorganized States, a special dispensation may be granted ordering another ballot taken immediately.

Section 4. A Klansman who presents the name of an applicant

278

APPENDIX

for membership in this Order must know the applicant personally and be familiar with his qualifications according to this Constitution and Laws. All members of a Klan must faithfully guard the portal of the Invisible Empire so that no person not qualified to enter therein shall be admitted.

Section 5. In the event a petitioner or an applicant is denied membership in this Order, the sum of his Klectokon shall be immediately returned to him by the Kleagle, if same was collected by him, or by the Kligrapp of the Klan if same was paid into the Klan.

Section 6. All actions of a Klan in rejecting an applicant for membership, as to the votes cast, and by whom objections were made, are a positive secret of this Order; members who have knowledge of same and divulge or intimate in the slightest degree or cause such knowledge to be in any way communicated to any person not a member, shall be at once banished from the Invisible Empire for the violation of his oath on the ground of treason.

Section 7. When the required number of charter petitioners have been obtained in a community where a Klan is to be located, the Kleagle will immediately forward a regular petition for the issuance of charter to the Imperial Wizard through regular channels. Such petition must give the name selected for that Klan, time of the meetings of regular klonklave and must be signed by the Kleagle in charge or the officers, giving the address of that Klan.

Section 8. The Klan charter shall contain the following text:

IMPERIAL PALACE INVISIBLE EMPIRE KNIGHTS OF
THE KU KLUX KLAN, INCORPORATED.

TO ALL WHO READ AND RESPECT THESE LINES, GREETING:

WHEREAS, the Imperial Wizard has received a petition from the following named citizens of the Invisible Empire
....
....
et al., praying for themselves and others and their successors to be instituted a Klan of the Order under the name and number

THE CHALLENGE OF THE KLAN

of ————— ....
Klan Number ...., Realm of .... and
same to be located at .... in the county of
.... State of...........
.................................., United States of America,
and they having given assurance of their fidelity to this Order
and their competency to render the service required, and their
ready willingness to take upon themselves and their successors
the duties and responsibilities thereof, and their serious determined purpose to rightly use and not abuse the powers,
privileges and prerogatives conferred on them as such, and be
faithful and true in all things committed to them;

Now know ye that I, the Imperial Wizard of the Knights of
the Ku Klux Klan, on this the .... day of
.... month of the Year of our Lord,
19————; and on the .... day of the ....
Week of the .... Month of the Year
of the Klan ...., and in the ....
Cycle of the Third Reign of our reincarnation, under the authority possessed by me, do issue this Charter to the aforesaid
petitioners, their associates and successors, under the name and
number aforesaid, from the day and date hereon, and same is
effective from the date of its acceptance by said Klan as certified
below.

The said Klan is hereby authorized and empowered to do and
to perform all such acts and things as are prescribed by the
Kloran, Laws, Imperial Decrees, Edicts, Mandates and Usages
of the Order, and to enjoy all the rights, privileges and prerogatives authorized by the Constitution thereof; and all Klansmen are strictly enjoined to valiantly preserve and persistently
practise the principles of pure Patriotism, Honor, Klannishness
and White Supremacy, ever keeping in mind and heart the sacred
sentiment, peculiar purpose, manly mission, and lofty ideals and
objects of this Order, a devoted loyalty to their Emperor and
their Imperial Wizard—a steadfast obedience to the Constitution
of this Order, a faithful keeping of their "Oath of Allegiance,"
and a constant, unwavering fidelity to every interest of the Invisible Empire, to the end that progress, power, purpose and

APPENDIX

influence of Klankraft be properly promoted, the knowledge of the faithful, self-sacrificing service and noble achievements of our Fathers be not lost to posterity, and all those things for which this, our beloved Order, is founded to do and perform and to protect, and to preserve and to perpetuate, be diligently done and scrupulously maintained, and that they be blameless in preserving the grace, dignity and intent of this Charter forever.

I solemnly charge you to hold fast to the dauntless faith of our Fathers and to keep their spotless memory secure and unstained, and true to the traditions of our valiant sires, meet every behest of Duty, in all the relationships of life and living, promptly and properly, without fault, without fail, without fear and without reproach.

The Imperial Wizard has and holds the full and unchallengeable authority, right and power to cancel, suspend or revoke this Charter, and to annul all the rights, powers, prerogatives, and immunities conferred hereby, for the neglect or the refusal on the part of the said Klan to conform to and comply with the Kloran, Constitution, and Laws of this Order, and the Imperial Decrees, Edicts, Mandates, Rulings and Instructions thereof, or its failure to respect the usages of this Order as proclaimed by and maintained under the Imperial Authority of same.

In testimony whereof I, the Imperial Wizard of the Knights of the Ku Klux Klan, have caused to be affixed hereon the Great Imperial Seal of the Invisible Empire, and do hereunto set my hand and impress my official seal, and same is duly attested—"Non Silba Sed Anthar."

Done in the Executive Chambers of his Lordship, the Imperial Wizard, in the Imperial Palace, in the Imperial City of Atlanta, Commonwealth of Georgia, United States of America, on the day and date above written.

BY HIS LORDSHIP,

....,
IMPERIAL WIZARD, OF THE INVISIBLE EMPIRE, KNIGHTS OF THE KU KLUX KLAN:

....
IMPERIAL KLIGRAPP.

THE CHALLENGE OF THE KLAN

CERTIFICATE OF ACCEPTANCE:
This certifies that this Charter was read to and duly adopted by above named Klan, in session assembled, with all stipulations and conditions herein stated or implied, on the ....
day of ...., A. D. 19........AK..........
(Signed.)

....

Exalted Cyclops of Above Named Klan.
Witness)

....

Section 9. Upon the receipt of the charter, the Kleagle or the Provisional Exalted Cyclops shall notify, or cause to be notified, the members of that Klan to assemble at the earliest convenient time in klonklave, at which klonklave the charter shall be read and accepted by the Klan and a record made in the minutes of the Klan. The charter of the Klan is then closed and the Klan will proceed to elect its elective officers, exercising care to select officers who are competent and fitted for the respective offices. This done, the service of the Kleagle terminates with this Klan. The Klan proceeds at once to supply itself with a seal and with adequate and suitable by-laws for its government and the regulation of its affairs and for the rigid protection and interests of this Order within its Klanton.

Section 10. By-laws of the Klan shall not conflict with or be inconsistent with the Constitution and Laws of this Order, and after same have been prepared by the Klan they must be immediately sent to the Imperial Wizard or Grand Dragon to be approved and ratified by him, corrected and amended by him if necessary and upon his ratification such by-laws become effective as law for the regulation of that Klan.

Section 11. The charter of a Klan may be reopened by the Grand Dragon of a Realm or by the Imperial Wizard upon a request by the Klan, signed by its Exalted Cyclops and Kligrapp. When a charter is reopened, the Grand Dragon or the Imperial Wizard will provide a Kleagle for this Klan for work under their direction.

Section 12. The elective officers of a Klan shall hereafter be

282

APPENDIX

as follows: The Exalted Cyclops, president; Klaliff, vice-president; Klokard, lecturer; Kludd, chaplain; Kligrapp, secretary; Klabee, treasurer; Kladd, conductor; Klarogo, inner guard; Klexter, outer guard; Night-Hawk, in charge of candidates; and three Klokann, board of investigators, auditors and advisers, each of whom shall bear the title of "Klokan." These shall be known as the Exalted Cyclops and his twelve Terrors.

Section 13. The term of office for officers of a Klan shall be for twelve months or until their successors have been elected and installed. Officers of a Klan shall be nominated in the klonklave immediately preceding the anniversary (May 6th) day, and elected at the klonklave immediately succeeding the anniversary day, each year, and installed in the first klonklave in the month of July.

Section 14. An officer of a Klan elected and who is absent on the night of installation shall be installed at the next klonklave, and if he should be absent from this klonklave he shall be notified to be present at the next klonklave for installation; then if he fails to present himself and has no providential excuse, his office shall be declared vacant by the Exalted Cyclops and the Klan shall proceed to elect at that klonklave a member to fill that vacancy, and such member elected shall be installed at that klonklave.

Section 15. Officers-elect shall not in any case be installed unless their Klan dues are paid up to and including the calendar quarter of installation and their respective offices shall become vacated if, at any time, their Klan dues become in arrears, and no Klan installation of officers shall be recognized within the Invisible Empire as being official unless that Klan be in good standing with the Imperial Palace, Realm and Province offices.

Section 16. When a Klan becomes in arrears in payment of its Imperial, Realm or Provincial tax for a period of one hundred days, its several officers are automatically vacated, its members denied visiting privileges in other Klans, and its acts subsequent thereto are invalid unless the time is extended by the Grand Dragon in organized Realms or the Imperial Wizard in unorganized Realms, either of whom shall have the authority

283

to order a complete audit of this Klan's affairs at the expense of the local Klan. Such Klan shall not be entitled to representation in any Klonverse, Klorero or Imperial Klonvokation. It shall be the duty of all Grand Dragons of Realms and Great Titans of Provinces to file with the Imperial Kligrapp, at least ten days preceding the Klonvokation, a list of all Klans in their respective territories which have paid their Realm or Province tax, and the numerical strength of the individual Klans.

Section 17. Immediately upon the election of officers the Kligrapp shall transmit the names of officers-elect to the Great Titan of the Province for ratification. Upon ratifying such officers-elect, the Great Titan shall immediately forward a copy of the list, together with his ratification, to the Grand Dragon of that Realm, who shall in turn file a copy in his office and transmit a copy immediately to the Imperial Kligrapp. No officer-elect shall be inducted into office unless he be worthy and well qualified to fulfill the duties of that office and his election duly ratified by the Great Titan or Grand Dragon.

Section 18. Klan dues shall be paid in advance. A new member shall begin paying dues the month immediately succeeding the month in which he was naturalized. A member failing to pay his dues for three successive months shall be automatically suspended from the Klan and his name dropped from the roll and he shall be so reported in the next quarterly report. Upon the payment of his arrears he shall be automatically reinstated and shall be so reported by the Kligrapp in his next quarterly report.

Section 19. Each and every member naturalized in this Order must supply himself with a robe and helmet by sending, through his Kligrapp, his measurement and the required fee for same. This robe and helmet shall be his and his only just so long as he is a member of this Order in good standing. Upon his voluntarily quitting this Order, or his being suspended or banished, for any cause, he shall return to the Exalted Cyclops his robe and helmet without delay, along with any other emblem, insignia or other property of this Order in his possession; all monies such member has paid were accepted as a guarantee of good faith, and same are forfeited by him.

284

APPENDIX

Section 20. A Klan under any and all circumstances shall accord full respect to its charter, and thereby strictly observe the Constitution and Laws, mannerisms, usages and Kloranic (ritualistic) regulations and requirements of this Order as same are promulgated by the Imperial Wizard; and shall give due respect and obedience to all Imperial, Realm and Provincial decrees, edicts, mandates, rulings and instructions issued by the said officers; and failure on the part of a Klan to do so shall be cause for revocation of its charter and the suspension of its entire membership from this Order.

Section 21. A Klan shall meet in klonklave at least once every month and gather promptly at the hour agreed upon. Six members of a Klan shall constitute a quorum for the transaction of any business at any regular klonklave.

Section 22. Special klonklaves may be held at any time whenever same are deemed necessary by the Exalted Cyclops or when he is requested to do so by twenty-five per cent. of the membership in good standing and ten per cent. in cases where the membership in good standing is greater than one thousand; provided, however, in no event under the provisions of this section shall the number required be less than one hundred in Klans having a membership in good standing greater than four hundred. If this meeting is called upon petition in accordance with the provisions of this section, forty per cent. of the membership in good standing at the time of such call shall constitute a quorum.

Section 23. In the event the charter of a Klan has been revoked or cancelled for any cause whatsoever, and in the event of disbandment of a Klan, whether it be a chartered or Provisional Klan, all monies of that Klan in the possession of any officer or member thereof shall automatically become the actual monies of the Imperial Treasury of this Order and same must be freely and promptly turned over, on demand, to the properly accredited officer who is authorized by the Imperial Wizard to receive same in the name of this Order; also all books, papers, manuscripts, Klorans, records, seal, Klan paraphernalia, regalia, robes, helmets and any and all other things used by the Klan, and all articles or things appertaining to this Order as may have

285

THE CHALLENGE OF THE KLAN

been used by or are in the possession of any individual member thereof.

Section 24. A Klan, or member of this Order shall not use the official costume or any part of same on any occasion outside the klavern without permission of the Grand Dragon in organized Realms, or the Imperial Wizard in unorganized States under penalty of forfeiture of their charter or banishment from this Order.

Section 25. No Klan or member shall use the name of this Order or any part thereof for any purpose that contravenes in any manner the laws of the land, that will reflect, or probably reflect, upon the reputation and good name, or compromise, or injure this Order, or any member thereof, in any way.

DUTIES OF KLAN OFFICERS.

ARTICLE XIX.

Section 1. EXALTED CYCLOPS: The Exalted Cyclops is the supreme officer of a Klan and its official head. He shall preside over the klonklaves and govern same with dignity, devotion and impartiality. He shall be faithful in the prompt and efficient discharge of every duty prescribed or implied, incumbent upon him, and fearless without respect to individual persons in the administration of the affairs of his office in promoting the welfare of this Order within the bounds of his Klanton, and he shall set a laudable example to all Klansmen, of patriotism, klannishness, benevolence, love, justice, honor and a devoted loyalty to this Order in every respect. He shall require a faithful observance on the part of all Klansmen within his Klanton of the Constitution, laws, usages, etc., of this Order, and all Imperial Realm or Province decrees, edicts, mandates, rulings and instructions, and seek to make vital and effective the principles, objects and purposes of this Order. He shall call the Klonklave to order promptly on the hour designated, if there be a quorum present, and see that his Terrors fill their respective offices in an acceptable manner. He shall diligently

286

APPENDIX

safeguard the sanctity and dignity of the charter of his Klan and suffer no encroachment thereon, nor any departure therefrom. He shall require the ritualistic work of the Kloran to be exemplified with the highest degree of perfection possible, and he shall do such other things as may be required of him by the Laws of this Order, the Kloran, the by-laws of his Klan, and faithfully execute all orders and special instructions of the Great Titan, Grand Dragon or the Imperial Wizard.

Section 2. KLALIFF: The Klaliff is the vice-president of his Klan, and he shall preside over the klonklave in the absence of the Exalted Cyclops. He shall preserve order during the deliberations of a klonklave, and otherwise assist the Exalted Cyclops in klonklave assembled and perform such other duties as may be required of him by the Exalted Cyclops, the Kloran and by-laws of his Klan.

Section 3. KLOKARD: The Klokard is the lecturer or instructor and the Klan censor or critic. He shall administer the oaths, deliver the Kloranic lectures, instruct in secret work, do those things commonly required of a critic, and perform such other duties as may be required of him by the Exalted Cyclops, the Kloran and the by-laws of his Klan. He shall be responsible for the proper performance of all ritualistic work within his Klan, and shall disseminate Klankraft throughout his Klanton.

Section 4. KLUDD: The Kludd is the chaplain of the Klan. He shall perform the duties peculiar to his sacred office, and such other duties as may be required of him by the Exalted Cyclops, the Kloran and the by-laws of his Klan. He shall be responsible for such musical programs as may be presented; and for the general spiritual welfare of his Klan.

Section 5. KLIGRAPP. The Kligrapp is the secretary and recording officer of the Klan. He shall keep an accurate and complete record of all the proceedings of his Klan assembled, and a correct and systematic record of its membership, and of the date each member was naturalized, etc., as required by the record book for that purpose. He shall make a report through the proper channels to the proper officers not later than the 10th of the month for the calendar quarter last past on the regular blanks therefor, and with his reports he shall remit to said

287

officer or officers all monies belonging to this Order, such as Imperial Tax, Realm or Provincial Tax, Klectokons, monies due for supplies and any and all other monies due and payable to said officers. He shall witness all requisitions made for any article or paraphernalia, regalia, jewelry, or other property of this Order, to be used by the Klan or a member thereof, and see that the required sum of money is sent therewith. He shall notify all members who are in arrears three months, and shall notify the Imperial Office of the arrears of a member for three months. He shall be the custodian of the seal of the Klan and shall impress it on all papers and documents requiring same, and perform such other duties as may be required of him by the Exalted Cyclops, the Kloran and the by-laws of his Klan.

Section 6. KLABEE: The Klabee is the treasurer of the Klan. He shall be the custodian of its funds, and shall receive from the Kligrapp all monies due to be turned over to him, giving his receipt for same, and keeping same apart from his personal funds and secure for the sole use of the Klan. He shall keep an accurate account of all monies received by him, and pay same out only on order of the Klan, signed by the Exalted Cyclops and the Kligrapp, except the monies due by the Klan to the Imperial Realm and Province Officers, which monies do not require action of the Klan, and make a faithful record of such disbursements. He shall make a complete and itemized report of his office to the Klan when same is requested by the Exalted Cyclops or the Klan, and shall perform such other duties as may be required of him by the Exalted Cyclops and the by-laws of his Klan.

Section 7. KLADD: The Kladd is the conductor of the Klan and the custodian of its paraphernalia and other properties. He shall conduct candidates for naturalization, collect the countersign and password at the opening of a klonklave, and perform such other duties as may be required of him by the Exalted Cyclops, the Kloran and the by-laws of his Klan.

Section 8. KLAROGO: The Klarogo is the inner guard of the Klan. He shall keep a diligent watch at the inner door and permit only those to enter the Klavern who are qualified or have the permission of the Exalted Cyclops. If he should be

APPENDIX

in doubt as to the qualifications of the one seeking admission, he must satisfy himself from the Klaliff or Kligrapp. He shall perform such other duties as may be required of him by the Exalted Cyclops, the Kloran and the by-laws of his Klan.

Section 9. KLEXTER: The Klexter is the outer guard of a Klan. He shall keep a diligent and faithful watch at the outer door, and allow no one to pass him from the outside except those who are qualified and have permission of the Exalted Cyclops. He shall observe from time to time the outside premises of the Klavern to see that no eavesdroppers or other persons are around who are liable to obtain information or knowledge concerning the acts or procedure of the klonklave. He shall in no case leave his post of duty unless summoned therefrom by the Exalted Cyclops, and even then, a substitute must be placed in his stead to watch until his return. He shall perform such other duties as may be required of him by the Exalted Cyclops, the Kloran and the by-laws of his Klan.

Section 10. NIGHT-HAWK: The Night-Hawk is the special courier of the Exalted Cyclops. He shall have charge of and shall entertain the candidate or candidates in the outer den of the klavern until he is signaled to enter the klavern at the beginning of the ceremony of naturalization. He shall carry the Fiery Cross in the ceremony and on all public exhibitions where same is used, and shall perform such other duties as may be required of him by the Exalted Cyclops, the Kloran and the by-laws of his Klan.

Section 11. KLOKANN: The Klokann is the Board of Auditors, Advisers and Trustees, and the investigating committee of the Klan. It shall be composed of three members, each of whom shall bear the title of "Klokan." It shall be their duty to audit the books and records of the Kligrapp and the Klabee in the month of June of each year, and oftener if so required by the Klan in writing. They shall see that all paraphernalia, regalia and other property of the Klan and of this Order is properly kept, and shall perform such other duties as may be required of them by the Exalted Cyclops and the by-laws of their Klan. Said Klokann may select such assistants as in their judgment seem necessary.

THE CHALLENGE OF THE KLAN

Section 12. An officer of a Klan who allows himself to get in arrears for three months, or who absents himself from three consecutive klonklaves without a providential excuse, or who fails to master his part of the kloranic work within sixty days after he is placed in office, shall forfeit all rights, prerogative♦ and honors of his office; the Exalted Cyclops must declare his office vacant and will at once appoint a successor thereto. If the Exalted Cyclops shall be guilty of negligence as above, the Klan in klonklave shall demand his resignation and whether tendered by him or not, they shall proceed to elect his successor at the following klonklave if he is not present to apologize to the Klan and take up his duties of office.

Section 13. The Grand Dragon or the Great Titan shall have the power to remove any officer of a local Klan for cause, but must immediately report said removal to the Tribunal of the Realm, whose duty it shall be to immediately pass on the correctness of his act. If he is sustained the Klan shall proceed to elect a successor to the officer removed; if he is not sustained, the officer removed resumes the duties of his office. This applies in Realms that have perfected Realm organizations. In all other jurisdictions this power is vested in the Imperial Wizard, who shall report same to the Imperial Kloncilium for review in the same manner as above set forth.

OFFENSES AND PENALTIES.

ARTICLE XX.

Section 1. Offenses against this Order shall be divided into two classes—major offenses and minor offenses.

Section 2. Major offenses shall consist of (1) treason against the United States of America; (2) violating the oath of allegiance to this Order or any supplementary oath or obligation thereof; (3) disrespect of virtuous womanhood; (4) violation of the Constitution or the laws of this Order; conspiring against the interest and prosperity of this Order or any Klansman in any way or being a party thereto, or being a party to any move,

290

APPENDIX

conspiracy or organization whose existence is antagonistic or injurious to or is an imitation of this Order; whose name, style or title is a colorable imitation of this Order; swearing allegiance to or otherwise becoming a citizen or subject of any nation, government or institution of any nature or classification whatsoever, or any ruler or potentate, prince or person of any court whatever that is foreign to or is inimical to the government of the United States of America and its established institutions, or aiding or abetting such government, nation, institution, ruler, potentate, prince or person against the interest, well-being or dignity of the United States of America or the distinctive institutions of its government; violating the by-laws of a Klan of this Order; excessive or habitual drunkenness; drunkenness or the drinking of intoxicating liquor or entering a klonklave in an intoxicated condition; the habitual use of profane language or vulgarity during a klonklave or during an assembly of Klansmen just prior thereto; (5) being responsible for the polluting of Caucasian blood through miscegenation, or the commission of any act unworthy of a Klansman; (6) the repeated commission of a minor offense shall in itself constitute a major offense.

Section 3. MINOR OFFENSES. Minor offenses shall consist of drunkenness, drinking of intoxicating liquor during a klonklave or on the premises thereof, entering a klonklave in an intoxicated condition, use of profane language or vulgarity during a klonklave or in an assembly of Klansmen just prior thereto, or committing any other act which might operate against the best interest of the Klan or Klansmen, refusal or failure to obey the mandates, rules, edicts and orders of the Exalted Cyclops or the Klan, or the failure or refusal on the part of any Klansman, upon demand by the Exalted Cyclops, to respond to any summons issued by him, unless he has a providential excuse; or failure or refusal to surrender his credentials when called for by the Exalted Cyclops.

Section 4. PENALTIES: All offenses enumerated above under the head of major offenses shall be tried and penalties assessed by the Tribunal hereinafter provided for. All offenses enumerated as minor offenses shall be heard and determined and penalties assessed by the Exalted Cyclops of the Klan. Penalties shall be of four classes, as follows: 1, Reprimand; 2, Suspension; 3, Banishment; 4, Extreme Penalty—banishment forever, and there shall be added thereto complete ostracism in any and all things by each and every member of this Order.

Section 5. A member who fails to respect the penalty imposed on another member shall receive the same penalty as if he himself were guilty of that offense.

Section 6. All charges against a Klansman, involving a major offense under the Constitution and Laws of the Knights of the Ku Klux Klan shall be in writing, specifying the acts complained of, which shall be submitted to the Klokann of the Klan of which the accused is a member, or in whose jurisdiction the offense was committed.

Section 7. Upon the filing of such charges the Klokann shall consider and investigate the same and take action thereon within thirty days from the time such charges are filed. The Klokann shall determine the sufficiency of the charges presented and the advisability of a trial as herein provided, and their action on such charges shall be final.

If the judgment of the Klokann is not unanimous, then the decision of a majority of the Klokann, when approved by the Exalted Cyclops, shall be final.

Section 8. Upon the filing of such charges the Klokann shall have the right in its discretion, through the Exalted Cyclops, to suspend the accused during the period of investigation of such charges or until his acquittal (if trial is ordered).

If, in the opinion of the Klokann, the charges presented constitute a minor offense, as herein defined, the same shall be referred to the Exalted Cyclops for such action as he shall deem proper.

Section 9. If the Klokann shall order a trial of the accused, the charges and specifications shall be published in regular klonklave by the Klaliff.

Section 10. The Exalted Cyclops shall in such event set the date of the trial which shall be not more than thirty days after report of the Klokann, and shall serve the accused with a copy of the indictment or charges not less than ten days before the date of the trial.

APPENDIX

Section 11. (a) The accused shall be tried before a Tribunal selected as follows: The Exalted Cyclops, Klaliff, Klokard and Kludd shall each select from the membership in good standing six Klansmen whose names shall be placed in some suitable receptacle and from this receptacle the Kladd, wearing a hoodwink, shall withdraw eight names, and the remaining sixteen Klansmen shall constitute the Tribunal whose attendance at the trial is compulsory. In the event any one or more of the sixteen Klansmen thus selected shall fail to appear, that number which do appear may select from the Klan body sufficient Klansmen to fill their places.

(b) In event of charges being presented against the Exalted Cyclops of a Klan, he shall immediately vacate his office and he shall remain out of office until the case against him is finally adjudicated. In such event the Klaliff shall immediately assume the office, duties and responsibilites of the Exalted Cyclops and shall appoint a Klaliff. The Klaliff in all respects shall be Exalted Cyclops in fact and the one appointed by him to the office of Klaliff shall be Klaliff in fact until the case against the Exalted Cyclops is finally adjudicated. In event the Exalted Cyclops so accused shall have been found guilty and duly penalized, the acting Exalted Cyclops and Klaliff shall remain in their respective offices until the end of the term, or until he shall have been reinstated. In the event charges are preferred against a Terror of a Klan he shall vacate his office immediately and shall remain out of office until the case against him has been finally adjudicated. Immediately upon his vacating office, the Exalted Cyclops shall appoint a substitute thereto and this substitute shall act in this office until the case against the Terror in question has been finally adjudicated. In the event the Terror in question is convicted and penalized, the substitute in his former office shall become the Terror in fact of that office unless or until the said Terror shall have been reinstated. In the event the Exalted Cyclops or any Terror of the Klan is accused and tried and acquitted, such Exalted Cyclops or Terror shall immediately resume his former office and proceed with the affairs of his office as before.

Section 12. Such Tribunal shall select one of their number as Triton, who shall preside, and one as Scribe, and the duty of the Scribe shall be to make a record of the proceedings, write the testimony of witnesses, or cause same to be done by a competent Klansman stenographer. Said Tribunal shall have authority and power to issue a summons directed to any Klansman, commanding him to appear and give testimony for or against the accused, and hear the charges and evidence and to render judgment in conformity with the laws of this Order and the evidence adduced.

Section 13. The Tribunal and the accused may take testimony touching the issues involved, except where Klan secrets and secret information of the Klan are involved, by interrogatories and cross interrogatories, first giving either party timely notice thereof, and such evidence when so taken may be received as evidence in the case and may be used by either party.

Section 14. On the date set for trial the accused shall be required to be present in person or by counsel (who shall be a Klansman in good standing), Providence alone preventing; and in the event of his failure or refusal to be present or represented by counsel the said Tribunal shall select a member in good standing in that Klan as counsel for the defense and proceed with the case and hear proof touching his guilt or innocence and render its decision in accordance with the laws of this Order and the evidence adduced at such trial; and said Tribunal in rendering its decision shall find whether or not service of the charges has been made upon the accused and notice of the time and place of hearing has been given to the defendant. Service of the time and place of the trial of the accused shall be made upon him in person or by registered letter, and a return card from the postoffice showing delivery thereof to such Klansman, coupled with an affidavit from the Night-Hawk of such Klan to the effect that a copy of the charges or indictment and a notice to the accused Klansman, specifying the time and place of trial, was placed in a letter in an envelope with proper postage and directed to such Klansman at his last known address, shall constitute service and notice on such Klansman.

Section 15. No evidence shall be offered at such trial except such as may be pertinent to the charges presented.

APPENDIX

Section 16. At a trial held under this article only the following may be present: (a) the Tribunal in full regalia of the Order; (b) the Prosecutor appointed by the Klokann; (c) the defendant and his representative or representatives; (d) witnesses who are Klansmen; (e) the Great Titan or his representative; (f) the Grand Dragon or his representative; (g) the Imperial Wizard or his representative; (h) a stenographer reporting the case, who must be a Klansman.

Section 17. At the conclusion of the evidence, the prosecutor and counsel for the accused shall have the right to argue the case to the Tribunal and the accused shall have the right to be heard in his own behalf, and at the conclusion of the arguments all persons except the Tribunal immediately shall retire.

Section 18. After fully considering the charges and evidence thereon, such Tribunal shall determine the guilt or innocence of the accused by written ballot. Twelve or more votes shall be necessary to convict or acquit.

Section 19. If the accused shall be found guilty, the Tribunal shall assess the penalty to be imposed and the Exalted Cyclops shall enforce the same, and such judgment shall be published by the Klaliff at the next regular klonklave.

Section 20. If the accused shall be acquitted, the Exalted Cyclops shall be notified thereof and such acquittal shall be published by the Klaliff at the next regular klonklave.

Section 21. If the Tribunal is unable to reach a decision as herein provided, then such Tribunal shall be discharged, another Tribunal composed altogether of different members from the former Tribunal shall be created as herein provided, who shall proceed to try the case as herein set forth.

Section 22. Should the accused be acquitted, a majority of the Klokann shall have the right to appeal from the judgment of the Tribunal and such majority of the Klokann shall also have the right to suspend the accused through the Exalted Cyclops until such appeal shall have been finally determined.

Section 23. Should the accused be convicted he shall have the right to appeal from the judgment of the Tribunal; but he shall remain suspended until such appeal shall have been finally determined.

THE CHALLENGE OF THE KLAN

Section 24. Notice of appeal shall be in writing signed by the party or parties appealing and filed with the Kligrapp of the Klan in which the accused was tried, not more than 15 days from the date the judgment of the Tribunal was published in regular klonklave.

Section 25. Upon the filing of such appeal, the Kligrapp, Triton and Scribe of the Tribunal shall, within 30 days, make up a complete transcript of the proceedings had upon the trial, which shall be duly certified to by the Kligrapp and forwarded by him immediately to the Grand Dragon of that Realm. Provided, however, that any member who shall be found guilty by a Tribunal in a Realm other than that in which he holds membership, shall have the right, at his option, to take his appeal to the Imperial Kloncilium instead of to the Grand Tribunal of the Realm where the trial is held.

Section 26. In States where Realm organization has not been instituted, the appeal shall be taken to the Imperial Kloncilium and a transcript of appeal filed with the Imperial Kligrapp in like manner as is provided in appeals to the Grand Tribunal of a Realm.

Section 27. In organized Realms the Grand Dragon shall annually select a Grand Tribunal composed of 12 Hydras or Giants, provided that for the first two years after a Realm is instituted the Tribunal may be composed of Hydras, Furies, Exalted Cyclops and Klaliffs.

Section 28. The Grand Tribunal shall meet at the annual meeting of the Klorero and at such other times as the Grand Dragon thereof may direct.

Section 29. The Grand Dragon shall designate one of said Grand Tribunal as Triton and he shall select his scribe therefor from the membership of the Grand Tribunal. The decision of nine or more members of said Grand Tribunal shall render judgment.

Section 30. Until Realm organization is instituted all appeals from judgments of the tribunal of the individual Klans in such states shall be reviewed by the Imperial Kloncilium whose judgments thereon shall be final.

Section 31. The procedure shall in all cases refer and apply

296

APPENDIX

to major offenses against the Order and shall in no sense alter or affect Sections 3 and 4 of Article XX of the Constitution and Laws.

Section 32. All judgments of the Tribunal shall be reported promptly by the Kligrapp of the Klan within 5 days to the Grand Dragon; or where a Realm organization has not been perfected, to the Imperial Kligrapp.

Section 33. Where banishment has been imposed, the Grand Dragon or the Imperial Kligrapp, as the case may be, shall so notify all Klans within the Realm where the case originated. Where the extreme penalty has been imposed, the Imperial Wizard shall decree, proclaim and publish same or cause the same to be done to all Klans throughout the Invisible Empire.

Section 34. In the event the preceding sections of this Constitution fail to provide for punishment of any Klansman for any of the offenses herein referred to, or for any other offense that is inimical to the best interest of this Order, the Imperial Wizard is hereby vested with authority and power to prefer charges against such Klansman in accordance with the provisions of this Article, or at his discretion to issue banishment order against such Klansman, who shall have the right of appeal to the Imperial Kloncilium for a period of 90 days after date of banishment. The Imperial Kligrapp shall publish the decree of banishment to Klans in the Realm in which such person held membership, or throughout the bounds of the Invisible Empire in accordance with the decree.

KU KLUX KALENDAR, KU KLUX KULLORS, ETC.

Article XXI.

Section 1. Hereafter the calendar of this Order, by which days, weeks, months and years shall be designated in all official documents, is as follows:

THE CHALLENGE OF THE KLAN

Days—	Weeks—	Months—
7. Desperate	5. Weird	12. Appalling
6. Dreadful	4. Wonderful	11. Frightful
5. Desolate	3. Wailing	10. Sorrowful
4. Doleful	2. Weeping	9. Mournful
3. Dismal	1. Woeful	8. Horrible
2. Deadly		7. Terrible
1. Dark		6. Alarming
		5. Furious
		4. Fearful
		3. Hideous
		2. Gloomy
		1. Bloody

YEAR OF THE KLAN: The year of the Klan (Anno Klan) begins with the month of May each year.

CYCLE: A cycle is twelve calendar months beginning with the month of December each year.

REIGN: The reign of Incarnation includes all time up to the American Revolutionary War. The first reign of our Re-incarnation dates from the beginning of the Revolutionary War and the establishment of our Government to the Organization of the Ku Klux Klan of the Reconstruction, in the year A. D. 1866. The second Reign of our Re-incarnation dates from the year A. D. 1866 to the year A. D. 1872. The third Reign of our Re-incarnation dates from the year A. D. 1915 on to the present and the future.

Section 2. The Kardinal Kullors of this Order, hereafter, shall be White, Crimson, Gold and Black. The secondary Kullors shall be Gray, Green and Blue. The Official Kullors of the Emperor shall be such as he may designate; those of the Imperial Wizard, Royal Purple. The significance and the mystery of these Kullors in the Invisible Empire shall be revealed Kloranically.

Section 3. There shall be four Kloranic Orders of this Order, namely: The Order of Citizenship or K-UNO (probationary); Knights Kamellia or K-DUO (primary Order of Knighthood);

298

APPENDIX

Knights of the Great Forrest or K-TRIO (The Order of American Chivalry); and Knights of the Midnight Mystery or K-QUAD (Superior Order of Knighthood and Spiritual Philosophies).

Section 4. These several orders of Klannish achievement and Kloranic advancement shall be communicated, and their Kloranic regulations, requirements and governments shall be established and promulgated by and in the discretion of the Emperor of this Order in the unfoldment of its philosophies and in the revelation of its spiritual mysteries.

ANNIVERSARY.

ARTICLE XXII.

Section 1. This Order was first organized and operated under the appellation of the Ku Klux Klan, or Invisible Empire, in the town of Pulaski, Tennessee, in the month of May, in the year Eighteen Hundred and Sixty-Six (1866), by six young men as a "social club." In the Year Eighteen Hundred and Sixty-Seven (1867) it was reorganized into a "regulative and protective organization" and as such it actively existed as a cohesive organization until about the year Eighteen Hundred and Seventy-Two (1872) at which time it voluntarily disbanded in pursuance of an order issued by its Grand Wizard-General Nathan Bedford Forrest. In the month of October, in the Year Nineteen Hundred and Fifteen (1915) it was resurrected, reconstructed and remodeled into its present incorporated form and character as a "historical, social, patriotic, military, benevolent, ritualistic, fraternal order or society" under its present appellation, by William Joseph Simmons, of Atlanta, Georgia, and thirty-three associates, three of whom were bona fide members in good standing of this Order when it disbanded as a regulative and protective Organization, as above stated.

Section 2. The anniversary date of this Order hereafter shall be the Sixth (6th) day of the Month of May each year.

Section 3. An anniversary celebration shall be held each year on the anniversary date in the City of Atlanta, Georgia, as the principal anniversary celebration of this Order, the concluding exercises of which shall be held, if possible, on the summit of Stone Mountain, near the City of Atlanta, Georgia, at midnight of the anniversary date.

BONDS.

ARTICLE XXIII.

Section 1. Each and every Kleagle, regularly appointed and commissioned by the Imperial Wizard, and the Kligrapp and Klabee of each and all subordinate jurisdictions shall give bond in whatever sum, and in whatever bond or surety company the Imperial Wizard may direct, and the premium for said bond must be paid by the jurisdiction or Klan for its Kligrapp and Klabee, and by the Kleagle or other officer bonded, except Imperial Officers, whose bond shall be paid from the Imperial Treasury.

ARTICLE XXIV.

Section 1. This Constitution may be amended by the Imperial Klonvokation, at any regular session thereof, provided that such proposed amendment be indorsed by the Klorero of three or more Realms, or such amendment be proposed by the Imperial Wizard. Such proposed amendment or amendments shall become a part of this Constitution when same has been passed by a two-thirds vote of the Klonvokation and also ratified by the Imperial Wizard; provided further that no amendment shall affect in any way the fundamental principles, objects, purposes and ideals of this Order, or the military character of its government.

Section 2. All laws and parts of laws in conflict herewith are hereby repealed and this Constitution shall go into effect immediately upon its adoption.

APPENDIX

CERTIFICATE OF ADOPTION.

THIS CERTIFIES that the above Constitution and laws of the Knights of the Ku Klux Klan, Incorporated, as duly authorized by the incorporators of said Corporation in session assembled on the Third day of July, A. D. 1916, AK-L, were duly adopted subject to ratification by the Imperial Wizard, by the Imperial Klonvokation of the Knights of the Ku Klux Klan, Incorporated, in its initial session, assembled on the Twenty-Ninth day of November, A. D. Nineteen Hundred and Twenty-Two, AK-LVI., in the City of Atlanta, Georgia. I officially declare and affirm that the text hereof is correct.

Atlanta, Georgia, November 29th, 1922.

Imperial Klaliff.
(Ex-Officio President of the Imperial Klonvokation.)

Attest:

Imperial Kligrapp,
(Secretary.)

CERTIFICATE OF RATIFICATION; AND PROCLAMATION.

To all Genii, Grand Dragons and Hydras, Great Titans and Furies, Giants, Exalted Cyclops and Terrors, and to all citizens of the Invisible Empire; in the name of the Valiant and Venerated dead, I affectionately greet you:

THIS CERTIFIES that the above Constitution and laws of the Knights of the Ku Klux Klan, Incorporated, as authorized, prepared and adopted by the Imperial Klonvokation of the Knights of the Ku Klux Klan, Incorporated, has been duly

301

submitted to me for ratification and proclamation; the same is hereby ratified and, therefore, I do

OFFICIALLY PROCLAIM

The same to be the Constitution and Laws of the Knights of the Ku Klux Klan, Incorporated, for the government of the Invisible Empire and all jurisdictions and Klans thereunder, and all persons therein, and to which all citizens thereof, Klansmen, members of this Order, have sworn an unqualified allegiance, and pledge in sacred sincerity, a constant inflexible obedience.

IN WITNESS WHEREOF, I, the Imperial Wizard of the Invisible Empire, Knights of the Ku Klux Klan, Incorporated, have caused the great Imperial Seal of the Knights of the Ku Klux Klan, Incorporated, to be impressed hereon, and I hereunto affix my official signature and seal on this the Twenty-Ninth day of the Eleventh Month of the Year of Our Lord Nineteen Hundred and Twenty-Two; and on the Doleful Day of the Weird Week of the Terrible Month of the Year of the Klan LVI, in the Seventh Cycle of the Third Reign of our Re-incarnation.

TO THE LOVERS of law and order, peace and justice, we send greetings; and to the shades of the Valiant, Venerated Dead, we gratefully and affectionately dedicate the Knights of the Ku Klux Klan.

Done in the executive chambers of His Lordship, the Imperial Wizard, in the Imperial Palace, in the Imperial City of Atlanta, Commonwealth of Georgia, United States of America, on the day and date above written.

"Non Silba Sed Anthar."
BY HIS LORDSHIP,

Imperial Wizard,
Knights of the Ku Klux Klan, Inc.

302

APPENDIX

(Imperial Seal)

(NEW ADMINISTRATION)

Attest:

H.H. Ramsey

Imperial Kligrapp,
Knights of the Ku Klux Klan.
(NEW ADMINISTRATION)